SHOULD YOU FIND YOURSELF CORNERING HARDER THAN A SPORTS CAR, TOWING A 3,500 KG LOAD, DESCENDING A 35° GRADIENT ON WET GRASS, OR CARRYING SEVEN PEOPLE IN SAFETY AND COMFORT, YOU'LL BE PLEASED YOU'RE IN A NEW DISCOVERY.

Not the snappiest headline you'll ever read. But then the New Discovery is 95% brand spanking new and we want to tell you all about it. So brace yourself. It's the only car in the world offering Active Cornering Enhancement (which keeps it flatter round corners than a sports car). It's the only 4x4 with seven forward facing seats all with three-point seat belts and full size head restraints. It has an advanced 5-cylinder turbo diesel engine, so you can carry out any of the manoeuvres above smoothly, quietly, powerfully and economically. And to top it all it's the only diesel 4x4 in which you could carry on doing it for 12,000 miles between services. But don't take our many words for it, test it yourself. 0800 110 110. www.landrover.co.uk

NEW DISCOVERY

Warranty extends to 3 years or 60,000 miles, whichever comes first. No mileage limit in the first year after purchase. Subject to manufacturer's terms and conditions. Extended warranty available in the UK only.

Want to manoeuvre confidently?

Our Practical Caravanning Courses and Caravan Manoeuvring Courses are designed especially for you by experienced caravanners to help you enjoy your caravanning more confidently.

"A very good course, once shown is better than ten times read" R.A.H., Sussex

The Caravan Manoeuvring Course is more compact and suitable for the caravanner who already knows and conforms to the Caravan Code, but has difficulty in reversing an outfit with confidence.

"An excellent Course which I shall definitely recommend to friends" Ms J.J. Powys

Practical work is provided by professional instructors who have practical caravanning experience. The courses are open to members and non-members alike. For both courses there is an invaluable and detailed Course Handbook provided for future reference, plus a VHS Video Guide *Confident Caravanning.*

Caravans are provided. All you have to is do is arrive in a car fitted with a towing bracket, functional electric sockets and two outside mirrors wide enough to see either side of the caravan. You must possess a full Group B driving licence (provisional not accepted) and the car must be insured to tow a trailer caravan.

The Practical Caravanning Course is ideal for newcomers–although older hands invariably wish they had taken a course years ago–and covers instruction and practice in:

▲ understanding loading and how it affects towing

▲ hitching up and towing, safely and efficiently

▲ practice in manoeuvring an outfit forwards and backwards, easily and confidently

▲ simple technical information to encourage user checks

▲ everyday safety checks and the law affecting caravanners

THE CARAVAN CLUB

Other essential guides to safe driving also published by The Stationery Office include:

Roadcraft – The Police Driver's Handbook
(011 340 8587)

Roadcraft – The Police Driver's Handbook Video
(011 341 1308)

The Official Driving Manual
(011 552 1917)

To order or find out more about these or any other driving titles, telephone The Stationery Office customer service on 0870 600 5522

Author: Philip Coyne
Design and illustration: Bill Mayblin
Editor: Penny Mares
Research: Philip Coyne, Bill Mayblin
Cover photographs courtesy of Brink UK

The Police Foundation

The Police Foundation is an independent research
charity working to improve the effectiveness of
policing and the relationship between the police and
the communities they serve.

For further details of the Foundation's work and
publications contact:

The Police Foundation
1 Glyn Street
London SE11 5RA

Tel: 0207 582 3744
Fax: 0207 587 0671

UK Charity No. 278257

Printed in the United Kingdom for The Stationery
Office by Clifford Thames
TJ000114 C100 02/00

"Accidents"

After this book went to press,
the Association of Chief Police
Officers made a formal decision
to stop using the word
"accident" to describe road
traffic incidents involving injury
and/or damage. This decision
was prompted by Transport
Research Laboratory findings
indicating human error as a
cause of 95% of such incidents.

Towing
Roadcraft

THE ESSENTIAL TOWING HANDBOOK

The Stationery Office

Foreword

I welcome this publication, which should be essential reading for anyone using a vehicle for towing purposes. The information in the manual covers not only the legal requirements, but also gives sound advice, which will enable drivers to be better equipped to deal with the everyday situations faced when towing.

The tremendous growth in traffic volumes and the competing demands for road space in recent years has meant more than ever before that, as individuals, we must recognise our own responsibilities towards other road users.

To tow safely requires a high degree of skill, concentration and hazard perception. I believe the guidance in this manual, if acted upon, will greatly assist in improving road safety to the benefit of all road users.

I commend *Towing Roadcraft – The Essential Towing Handbook* to you.

Paul Manning
Assistant Commissioner
Chairman ACPO Traffic Committee

Acknowledgements

This first edition of *Towing Roadcraft* was initiated by The Police Foundation at the suggestion of the National Trailer and Towing Association and Brink UK.

The author and The Police Foundation would like to thank the following for their advice and assistance.

Steve Hanley of the Trailer and Towing Advisory Service and formerly of the National Trailer and Towing Association, who acted as technical consultant throughout the preparation of the book.

Professor Robert West for his contribution to the contents of the Introduction.

Christopher Rush of Brink UK, John Parsons of the Caravan Club and Brian Bates of the National Trailer and Towing Association for their comments on the first draft.

The many individuals, organisations and companies who gave so freely of their time and advice during the research for the book.

Contents

Introduction

Scope of this book

More than 15% of vehicles are fitted with a towbar. These towbars are used to tow caravans, horseboxes, boat trailers, box trailers and general purpose trailers. Caravans may appear to be the commonest type of trailer but in fact are only 20% of the trailer market. *Towing Roadcraft* reflects this; it contains advice for all users of light trailers. It covers unbraked trailers up to 750kg maximum gross weight, and braked trailers up to 3500kg maximum gross weight (EC categories 01 and 02 trailers). Heavier trailers come under different regulations and are outside the scope of this book.

A note on terminology

Throughout this book the word trailer is used to refer to all types of trailer, including caravans. Where advice relates to a specific type of trailer, this is made clear in the text. The word vehicle is used to mean the towing vehicle. Outfit is used for the combined vehicle and trailer, which is also called a combination.

Towing safely

This Introduction deals with a key aspect of skilful towing – your attitudes to driving. It focuses on the mental aspects of driving, and looks at how attitudes and concentration affect your towing. This is because the bedrock of safe towing is your attitude to risk, safety and the need for hazard awareness. No matter how well balanced your outfit is, if you drive without regard to the safety of yourself and other road users you put lives and property at risk.

Driving attitudes and towing

Research evidence shows that attitudes affect towing safety, but developing appropriate attitudes is not simple. It depends on recognising that attitudes are important, and on making a personal commitment to changing unsafe attitudes. The first part of the chapter looks at what makes a good driver of an outfit. It goes on to look at the pattern of traffic accidents in Great Britain, and at what the research evidence tells us about who is at greatest risk of having an accident. Understanding this evidence can be an important step in recognising and changing inappropriate attitudes.

What makes a good outfit driver?

Drivers who are good at towing are both calm and efficient. These qualities depend on:

- a good level of concentration
- accurate observation
- matching the outfit's speed and direction to the situation
- awareness of the risks inherent in particular road and traffic situations
- acting to keep identified risks to a minimum
- awareness of their own limitations and those of the outfit and the roads
- skilful use of vehicle controls and towing techniques
- attitudes that contribute to road safety.

It is not simply the speed of your reactions that determines whether you are safe but your ability to identify and respond to hazards. Quick reactions to simple stimuli such as noise and light do not, on their own, reduce accident risk. Young, inexperienced drivers typically have very fast reactions to simple stimuli but have slow reactions to traffic hazards.

The ability to detect hazards is learnt like any other skill and depends partly on experience. More experienced towers develop a sensitivity to the early indications of possible trouble. When risks arise they monitor them at a subconscious level in readiness to respond quickly if the situation develops dangerously. Because they are more aware of potential danger they are more alert while towing, and this helps to sustain their concentration. (For more on concentration and attention see below.)

Traffic accidents

Like most drivers, drivers of outfits think they are both safer and more skilful than the average driver – but we cannot all be right. In more than 90% of traffic accidents, human error is the cause. Accidents do not just happen, they are the consequence of unsafe driving practices. Towing safety cannot be thought of as an add-on extra; it has to be built into the way you drive.

Traffic accidents account for:

- almost half of all accidental deaths in Britain
- nearly a quarter of all adult deaths under 30, whether accidental or not – they are the largest single cause of death for young adults.

Your likelihood of having an accident

Average drivers cover about 10,000 miles a year and have a one in seven chance of an accident during that time. Some types of driver are more at risk than others:

- those travelling more miles than average per year
- younger drivers, especially men
- inexperienced drivers.

Drivers of outfits towed by a car or light commercial vehicle have about 1500 accidents involving personal injury each year. This represents about 0.5% of the personal injury accidents involving cars and light commercial vehicles. Caravans are involved in about 300 personal injury accidents each year.

The apparently low percentage figure for trailer accidents should not be regarded as a source of comfort. The figure reflects the low level of trailer use in the driving population at large, and the low average annual mileage of most trailers. Even at this level it means that vehicles towing light trailers are involved in more than four personal injury accidents every day in Britain.

If you start towing in your thirties or forties you may think that none of the above risk factors apply to you. But think again about inexperience. Towing a trailer is very different from driving solo. Your outfit is longer, slower, takes longer to accelerate and brake, and handles very differently from a solo vehicle. Also the hazards that you face are different. You may be an experienced solo driver but you are a novice as far as towing is concerned. Recognise that it will take you some time to become as accomplished an outfit driver as you are a solo driver.

What are the likeliest sorts of accidents?

We can also tell from the statistics which are the commonest types of accident:

- about a third of all accidents are rear end shunts – where one vehicle crashes into the back of another
- a quarter of all accidents are caused by one vehicle crossing another vehicle's priority
- around one sixth of all accidents involve a loss of steering control.

The overwhelming majority of accidents take place at a junction. Drivers of outfits need to take special care at junctions because of their greater length and reduced acceleration.

Do we learn from our mistakes?

Those at risk

The evidence shows that we are not good at learning from our mistakes. Even after taking account of age, sex, annual mileage and driving experience, some people are consistently more at risk than others:

- if you have had an accident in the last three years, you are twice as likely as normal to have an accident in the next three years
- if you have an accident for which you are partly responsible, you are four times more likely than normal to have a similar accident in the next year.

We know that drivers tend to repeat the same type of accident. If you have an accident or near miss, think very carefully about what you could have done to avoid the situation. If you do not learn from your experience you are likely to make the same mistakes.

Following too close

The practice of driving too close to the vehicle in front gives a valuable insight into the causes of accidents. Because errors go unpunished – that is, they are not always followed by an accident – they develop into bad habits which increase the risk of an eventual accident.

Driving too close to the vehicle in front is one of the commonest causes of vehicle accidents. There is a greater risk for drivers towing a trailer because of the reduced braking efficiency of outfits. If the driver behind is too close, increase the distance between yourself and the vehicle in front. It will allow you to brake more gently, giving the vehicle behind more time to stop.

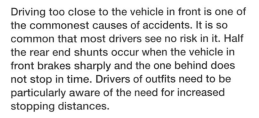

Driving too close to the vehicle in front is one of the commonest causes of accidents. It is so common that most drivers see no risk in it. Half the rear end shunts occur when the vehicle in front brakes sharply and the one behind does not stop in time. Drivers of outfits need to be particularly aware of the need for increased stopping distances.

Resistance to learning from experience

Research shows that most drivers involved in an accident do not accept that they had any responsibility for the accident. If you believe that you did not contribute to an accident, you will not learn from it. Your driving technique, and the faults that led to the accident, will remain unchanged.

To tow safely, you have to recognise your own resistance to accepting responsibility, and take steps to overcome it. The first step is to recognise that we all, including yourself, have a resistance to learning. The next step is to recognise every near miss and accident as an opportunity to re-evaluate and improve your towing technique.

Once we have learnt to do something routinely we are very reluctant to alter that routine, whatever the evidence that it does not work.

How your attitudes affect your ability to tow

Drivers' attitudes to other road users, speed and risk taking are a good guide to their likelihood of having an accident. Later in this section there is an opportunity for you to try two attitude tests used in research studies.

Attitudes to other road users

Towing safely depends on constructive attitudes and consideration for other road users. There is already a great deal of potential conflict on the roads without adding to it by acting aggressively or disregarding the interests of other road users. Such behaviour increases the stress levels of other road users and increases the risk of accidents. Many road users become unnecessarily angry when others interrupt their progress. Even behaviour that is perfectly reasonable may be a source of irritation.

Drivers of outfits should be aware that their size and relatively slow progress may cause other drivers to react angrily. You can reduce the risk of accidents for yourself and everyone else by being more tolerant and by avoiding actions which create unnecessary stress. Drivers who show consideration for other road users are less likely to become involved in accidents.

Attitudes to speed

The speed at which you drive is one of the most important factors in determining your risk of having an accident. Driving too fast is probably the factor that puts drivers at greatest risk of death. The faster you go, the greater the risk of losing control of your outfit, the less chance of taking avoiding action, and the greater your risk of having an accident. Speed is largely a matter of choice – the occasions when it is absolutely necessary to drive fast are fairly limited. Good towing requires you to drive at a speed that is safe for your outfit and safe for the conditions.

Attitudes to risk taking

Whenever you tow there is always some element of risk but your attitudes can greatly influence the degree of risk involved. People whose attitudes lead them to take more risks do in fact have more accidents. Attitudes which predispose you to risk are:

- enjoying the thrill of danger
- enjoying impressing other road users
- a disregard for personal safety
- the illusion of control, or overestimating your ability.

Young, inexperienced drivers run the greatest risk of accidents because they have a greater tendency to seek risk and disregard danger. They also see less risk in many traffic situations than more experienced drivers.

As a group, drivers who ignore the law and tow their outfits in a risky way underestimate their likelihood of having an accident. As we have seen, risk-taking drivers have a higher chance of being involved in an accident than other drivers.

Many drivers take risks to impress other people – for example, young male drivers tend to drive faster when they have a young male passenger than when alone or with a female passenger.

Many drivers suffer from the illusion of control. They overestimate their ability to cope with the demands of traffic when they are driving. This distorts their assessment of risk.

Time pressure and towing safely

Drivers who feel their journey is urgent, because of time pressure or because of the purpose of the journey, respond less safely to hazards and take more risks than other drivers. A sense of urgency does not give you the right to take risks.

Holiday pressures

Always allow yourself adequate time when towing a trailer. This is particularly relevant to towers of recreational trailers, such as caravans, on holiday. Holidaymakers often have to work to a set schedule for arriving at their campsite or embarking for a crossing. But congestion is often worst during the main holiday times resulting in unforeseen delays. Allow for unpredictable hold-ups by building a generous safety margin into your timings. The need to catch a ferry is no justification for driving too fast or taking other risks that might cause injury or death. Alternatively, plan your journeys for times when congestion is at a minimum, but still allow adequate time.

Road tantrums

Drivers who allow themselves to get into a rage with other drivers are no longer capable of realistically assessing driving risks. They ignore normal risk factors such as wet roads, heavy traffic or urban conditions, and the result is a significant increase in accidents. The congestion, danger and frustration of current driving conditions provide fertile grounds for emotional conflict with other drivers. We need to recognise this and take active steps to disengage our emotions from the driving situation. The key to this is to concentrate on the driving task in hand rather than emotional engagement with other drivers. Do not get into personality conflicts with other drivers. Be dispassionate about incidents and concentrate on your driving.

Other causes of risk taking

Rash decision making also increases the risk. If you do not consider all the implications of your decisions, your actions are unpredictable and you fail to take account of traffic conditions.

Emotional mood and accident risk

Drivers commonly express their feelings in the way that they drive, and this can be very dangerous. Drivers who have recently had an argument behave more aggressively than normal and drive too fast and too close to the vehicle in front. American research shows that there is a greater risk of an accident during times of stress such as during divorce proceedings. Drivers of caravans and other recreational trailers should plan their departure carefully to avoid the stress commonly associated with the start of holiday trips. By preparing as fully as possible before the day of departure and by allowing adequate time for the trip, much can be done to avoid unnecessary stress.

Traffic delays are a common source of stress and frustration, and are frequently encountered by recreational towers. Many drivers release this frustration by driving more aggressively and by taking more risks. If you are able to recognise this as a problem and can find other ways of coping with the stress you will improve your driving. Taking your journey one incident at a time and accepting that you may not be able to keep to your schedule are important ways of reducing stress.

Most people are reactive; if they encounter another driver with a courteous attitude and an obvious concern for safety, they are encouraged to adopt a similar approach. By driving safely and courteously we can influence the behaviour of other motorists for the better.

Changing unhelpful attitudes

Develop positive attitudes

We have now looked at driving attitudes that increase the risk of accidents. Positive attitudes that help reduce accident risk are:

- a tolerance and consideration for other road users
- a realistic appraisal of your own abilities
- an awareness of your vulnerability as a driver
- a high degree of care for your own safety, for your passengers and for other road users.

You need to be able to recognise your own limitations and to set aside personal goals in the interests of safety – an example would be restraining yourself from reacting aggressively to another road user's aggressive behaviour. You need to make decisions carefully, to take full account of the traffic conditions and to avoid acting in an unpredictable way.

Check your own attitudes

Use the questionnaire below to assess your attitude to driving.
Try and be as truthful as possible – the more truthful you are
the more accurate the result will be.

Attitudes to driving

Listed below are some statements about driving. For each one show how far you
agree or disagree with it by putting a circle around the appropriate number. For
example circling 1 means that you strongly agree with the statement.

	Strongly agree	Agree	Neither agree nor disagree	Disagree	Strongly disagree
Decreasing the speed limit on motorways is a good idea	1	2	3	4	5
Even at night time on quiet roads it is important to keep within the speed limit	1	2	3	4	5
Drivers who cause accidents by reckless driving should be banned from driving for life	1	2	3	4	5
People should drive slower than the limit when it is raining	1	2	3	4	5
Road users should never overtake on the inside lane even if a slow driver is blocking the outside lane	1	2	3	4	5
Penalties for speeding should be more severe	1	2	3	4	5
In towns where there are a lot of pedestrians, the speed limit should be 20 mph	1	2	3	4	5

When you have finished add up the numbers which you have circled. If you scored less than 15 you tend to
agree with the statements. If you scored between 15 and 21 you are generally neutral or average. If you
scored more than 21 you tend to disagree with the statements. Drivers who tend to disagree with these
statements turn out to have approximately five times the accident risk of those who agree.

If the table shows you to have a high accident risk, you need to think seriously about what you can do to change the attitudes that put you at risk. The next section analyses some of these attitudes and suggests how you might begin to tackle them.

Acknowledge resistance to change

Most drivers would accept that developing a safety conscious attitude is important, but a problem exists because we believe our own attitudes are right and are reluctant to accept evidence that we need to change them. Attitude to speed is a key area where there is often resistance to change. To assess your own attitude to speed, complete the questionnaire that follows.

Driving speed

For each question put a circle around the number corresponding to the answer that applies to you during your normal everyday driving (not during emergency driving).

	Never or very infrequently	Quite infrequently	Infrequently	Frequently	Always
How often do you exceed the 70 mph limit during a motorway journey?	1	2	3	4	5
How often do you exceed the speed limit in built up areas?	1	2	3	4	5
How often do you drive fast?	1	2	3	4	5

When you have finished, you can add up the numbers which you have circled. If you scored less than 7, you tend to speed infrequently. If you scored between 7 and 12 you tend to speed a little more frequently. If you scored more than 12 you tend to speed often. Drivers who indicate on this questionnaire that they speed often have about three times the accident risk of those who speed infrequently.

If you have scored more than 12 on the questionnaire do you agree that you have a greater risk of causing an accident? Or do you think there are special circumstances in your case?

If you think there are special circumstances, which explain your score, make a list of them and look at them critically. Are your explanations genuine or do they spring from a reluctance to accept change?

Try discussing your reasons with a friend or someone who knows you well to achieve a more objective assessment of your explanations.

Many drivers who are fast, aggressive and inconsiderate are quite happy with the way they drive and do not accept that it is unsafe. They tend to think that their behaviour is more common than it really is, and that it is the result of external pressures rather than their own choice. These rationalisations create barriers to attitude change, and need to be overcome if change is to happen.

Recognise your own vulnerability

If you have unsafe attitudes towards towing, and can recognise this, the next step is to make safety your main concern. Identify which of your views bolster unsafe attitudes to driving and how you can change them. Key unsafe attitudes are:

- a false sense of personal invulnerability
- an illusion of control.

These prevent us from accepting that the risks apply to us as well as to other people.

Critical self-awareness – the key to towing skill

Acknowledging the need to change attitudes is difficult because the evidence is statistical and most people trust their own experience rather than statistics. If you are a fast or aggressive driver, you may not make the connection between your attitudes and the way you tow even if you have been in an accident. Research has shown that those involved in an accident overwhelmingly blame the road conditions or other drivers rather than themselves for the accidents that they cause. This helps to explain why drivers repeatedly make the same mistakes and have the same kinds of accidents.

A safe approach to towing requires you to take a cool look at the facts, to be prepared to discard inappropriate attitudes and to develop a critical awareness of your own attitudes and capabilities.

The key steps to achieving this self-awareness are:

- acknowledging that attitudes affect your driving
- being aware of your own attitudes and recognising that they affect your risk of having an accident
- recognising that you are vulnerable
- making safety your primary concern whenever you tow (and in your other driving)
- considering your own experience of near misses or accidents and what you can learn from them.

Concentration and alertness

Concentration and alertness are essential for safe towing. This section looks at the factors which can help or hinder them.

Our ability to handle information about the environment is limited. We cope with this by selective concentration on parts of the environment and paying less attention to the rest. This is important in driving because we react most quickly to things happening in the part of the environment on which we are concentrating.

One way of seeing this is to imagine your field of view as a picture – you can see the whole picture but you can only concentrate on one part of it at a time.

If you concentrate your vision on a small area you are less aware of the whole picture.

If you concentrate on different areas of the environment in turn, you become more aware of the picture as a whole.

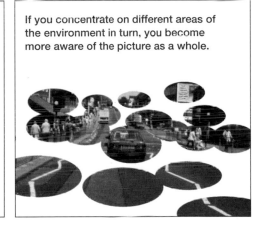

Scanning the environment

Drivers who can rapidly scan the whole environment looking for different kinds of hazards have a lower risk of accident than drivers who concentrate on one area. There are several ways to develop your ability to do this:

- move your eyes around and look in all directions, including the mirrors
- look for hazards in any shape or size and from any direction
- develop your sensitivity to the variety of possible hazards in different towing situations – this depends on learning, experience and a commitment to developing this awareness.

Looking but not seeing

What we see depends largely on what we expect to see. You may have experienced, at one time or another, pulling out and narrowly missing a bicycle coming from the direction in which you have just looked. Errors of this type are common because drivers are generally looking for cars or lorries but not for smaller objects such as bicycles or motorcycles, which they fail to see. When we concentrate, we don't just look at a particular part of a scene, we look for particular types of objects in that scene. We find it easier to detect objects that we expect to see, and react more quickly to them. Conversely we often fail to see objects that we do not expect to see.

In looking for cars and lorries, drivers can become blind to smaller, less expected road users.

Developing your awareness of towing hazards

Some processing of information goes on at a subconscious level but a prompt can summon our attention to it. An example is the way we prick up our ears when we hear our name mentioned. Experienced drivers rapidly and automatically switch their attention to events happening outside their field of focus because they have a subconscious or instinctive understanding of the implications of particular traffic situations.

In the following chapters of *Towing Roadcraft* we look at many examples of traffic situations and the towing hazards that occur in them. You may wonder whether so many examples are necessary, but their purpose is to increase your understanding of the potential hazards in each situation. The aim is to 'pre-sensitise' your awareness so that when you encounter a situation you already know what hazards to look for and can respond to them more quickly.

Alertness

Alertness determines the amount of information you can process – it can be thought of as mental energy and its opposite is tiredness or fatigue. Alertness depends on many things, but with routine tasks like towing, it tends to decrease with time spent on the task. Alertness also depends to some extent on your personality. Extroverts (outgoing people who need a lot of external stimulation) are probably more susceptible to fatigue than introverts (inward looking people who avoid high levels of stimulation).

To tow well you need to stay alert – ready to anticipate, identify and respond to hazards. But most towing is routine, it places few demands on our abilities and the risk of accidents from moment to moment is small. This relatively low level of stimulation makes it easy to lose concentration, and we need to take active steps to maintain it. In busy urban traffic, the demands of driving may be sufficiently stimulating, but on long journeys on motorways or rural roads other forms of stimulation are needed.

Alertness and anxiety

Alertness depends on your level of anxiety, and there is an optimum level of anxiety for any task. A small amount of anxiety arising from a clear understanding of the risks involved can help to maintain alertness and readiness to respond. No anxiety at all dampens your responsiveness and decreases your speed of reaction. Too much anxiety can result in failure to process information and respond appropriately.

You can help yourself to stay alert by:

- consciously assessing the current level of risk
- constantly updating your assessment
- talking yourself through the risks of the traffic situation.

If you actively maintain your awareness of the risks in this way, it will help you to keep anxiety at an optimum level, and you will be less likely to neglect a potentially dangerous situation.

Fatigue

Fatigue is related to total activity time and not just to the time spent driving. If you are tired before you start a journey, you are much more at risk from fatigue during the journey. Towing trailers can put you at greater risk of fatigue because of the lower speeds, high levels of concentration, and lengthy journeys undertaken by recreational trailer owners. Professional drivers are also at risk because professional and social pressures encourage them to continue driving beyond what they know is their safe limit.

Health, medication and emotional state

You should not drive an outfit when you feel unwell. This is particularly important on motorways because of the dangers of high-speed accidents and the limited opportunities to stop if you feel ill. Medication is a common source of drowsiness, so if you are taking medicine follow any advice on the container or given by your doctor about driving. Your emotional state affects your ability to recognise hazards, to take appropriate decisions and to implement them efficiently. If you are emotionally distressed you should be aware of the effect that it is likely to have on your ability to tow.

Monotonous conditions

Towing for long periods in monotonous conditions such as low-density traffic, fog or at night or on a motorway reduces stimulation and promotes fatigue.

How to combat fatigue when towing

To reduce the risk of fatigue:

- make sure that you are not tired before you start towing
- adjust your seat to make your driving position comfortable; bad posture causes muscular fatigue which in turn causes mental fatigue.
- take adequate rest breaks (see below).

At night, dazzle and constantly changing conditions of visibility quickly result in tiredness. Night driving puts heavy demands on the eyes and any slight eyesight irregularity can cause stress and fatigue. If you find you are suffering from fatigue unexpectedly, especially at night, it is wise to get your eyes tested. As we age, most of us develop eyesight irregularities and can benefit from correctly prescribed glasses.

An unstable outfit causes fatigue: do everything that you can do to make your outfit as stable as possible.

Rest breaks

Taking rest breaks is essential to recover from the onset of fatigue. A rest break at least every two hours is recommended. It appears that most people need a rest break of at least 20 minutes to restore alertness. On long journeys you should plan a series of rest breaks, but recognise that each successive break will give less recovery than the one before. Physical activity helps recovery, so include some walking as well as sitting down and relaxing during planned breaks.

People over 45 need to be aware that they are more at risk of and recover less quickly from fatigue than younger drivers.

Biological rhythms

Alertness is reduced if you drive at times when you would normally be asleep or if you have not had a normal amount of sleep. It also varies with the time of day.

● Our reactions tend to be slightly faster in the early evening than in the morning.

● There seems to be a dip in alertness after the midday meal.

● The greatest risk of fatigue related accidents is between the hours of midnight and 8.00 am.

If you feel drowsy, if your eyelids are heavy and the rear lights ahead start to blur, you must do something to stop yourself falling asleep. Take a rest as soon as it is safe.

Learning safe towing skills

Safe towing habits depend on appropriate attitudes and on appropriate skills in hazard perception and outfit control. You will find it easier to improve and develop your skills if you have some understanding of how we learn skills and of what role instruction plays in the learning process.

Skilled performance of any task depends on three main elements:

● rapid and accurate perception of the relevant information

● rapid choice of an appropriate response

● accurate execution of the chosen response.

Attitude, as we have seen, is important in identifying what is relevant and in selecting an appropriate response. Speed and accuracy, the other attributes of skill, depend on practice and feedback.

Practice and feedback

The two basic requirements for skill development are practice, and feedback on the effect of our actions. The better the feedback the better the learning. Complicated skills such as towing are built up from smaller skill elements. Early in practice we need detailed feedback on each of the elements, but later, as the different elements of a skill are put together and become automatic, we are less and less aware of our individual actions. This has two results: firstly, each decision covers a bigger task so that fewer decisions are needed; secondly, our actions become smoother and less hurried.

When you have mastered the basic controls and skills required to tow a trailer, you can devote more of your attention to the road and traffic conditions. This improves your anticipation and response to hazards: key areas of advanced driving. Your performance becomes more relaxed and efficient, making it appear that you have all the time in the world.

Throughout this book you will find many routines, such as the system of driving control, designed to improve your ability to tow. At first they will put heavy demands on your attention and thinking time, but as you get used to them, they will become second nature. Learning these skills mirrors the process by which you learnt the basic driving skills to pass your test. At first, activities like changing gear or turning round in the road required all your attention, but with practice they became automatic, allowing you to devote more of your attention to reading the road.

Towing instruction

Training accelerates your learning, enabling you to develop skills that you might otherwise never possess. There are many organisations able to provide training in towing, especially the major caravanning and trailer organisations. Training can improve your hazard perception by making you aware of the potentially dangerous situations in different traffic environments, and by giving you practice in detecting them. But it is important for you to take an active role in developing your own learning.
We each learn differently, and you alone can identify which methods work best for you. To learn effectively you need to have the right balance between instruction and practice. Instruction can draw your attention to parts of a task or ways of doing things but practice is the only way in which skills become automatic and readily available when you need them.

Maintaining your trailer

Currently there is no obligatory maintenance and safety test for light trailers equivalent to the MOT test for vehicles. This places responsibility for maintaining the safety and condition of trailers fully on the owners of the trailers. Trailers generally have few mechanical parts, but the coupling system, braking system, electrical system, and suspension, wheels and bearings all require regular inspection and maintenance. There is advice on maintenance throughout this book and a specific section on it at the end of the book. It is important that you follow the advice.

Chapter 1

Towing trailers and the law

The law controls towing trailers. Drivers are required to hold the appropriate licence; towing vehicles, trailers, towbars, couplings and drawbars have to meet set standards; the size and weight of towing vehicles and trailers are restricted individually and in combination; and specific road traffic regulations govern the use of trailers on the highway. This chapter sets out key regulations which control the use of trailers. Further practical advice on putting together a safe and stable outfit is contained in Chapter 2. This book should not be construed as a legal statement. The law affecting towing is in a constant state of evolution as a result of new regulations and court decisions. On any particular issue, you are advised to obtain a copy of the most recent regulations, available from The Stationery Office, and/or to seek advice from one of the organisations listed at the end of the book.

Driving licence requirements

Before towing a trailer of any description you must pass a category B theory and practical test. The size of trailer you can tow, and the combinations you can drive depend on your licence entitlement. Car drivers who passed their driving test before the beginning of 1997 are entitled to drive larger combinations than those who passed their test after this date. Drivers who passed their test after 1 January 1997 are required to pass additional tests to gain the necessary entitlements to drive larger combinations.

The information on page 21 sets out the entitlements for drivers who have passed the basic car test since 1 January 1997. This is followed by the entitlements for drivers who passed their test before this date. Contact the Driver and Vehicle Licensing Agency (DVLA) for information on categories of entitlement not covered here – this book covers categories B and B+E. You can find the number in the phone book.

Key terms

Before going any further it is important to be clear about the precise meaning of a number of key phrases commonly used when discussing trailers and towing:

Gross Train Weight (GTW): the maximum weight a vehicle can move on the road as stated by the manufacturer. It includes the vehicle's own MAM *(see below)* and the maximum weight of an attached loaded trailer. It is the same as the combined MAM.

Gross Vehicle Weight (GVW): the total weight that a trailer or vehicle is designed to carry. It consists of the weight of the trailer or vehicle and its load.

Kerbweight (KW): *there are two definitions of kerbweight. The first is the definition established in UK legislation, the second is the definition used in EU Directives.*

Kerbweight (KW): (as defined in Construction and Use Regulations 1986)
The weight of a vehicle as it leaves the manufacturer with a full tank of fuel, adequate fluids for normal operation (lubricants, oils, water etc), and its standard set of tools and equipment. It does not include the weight of the driver, occupants or load. For a trailer the KW is the unladen weight of the trailer.

Kerbweight (KW): (as defined by EU Directive 95/48/EC) the weight of a vehicle as it leaves the manufacturer with its fuel tank 90% full, all the necessary fluids for normal operation (lubricants, oils, water etc), a nominal driver weight of 68kg, and 7kg of luggage.

Maximum Authorised Mass (MAM): the maximum total weight that a vehicle is designed to carry. It is set by the vehicle manufacturer, and includes the vehicle weight and the load carried. It is the same as the older terms: permissible maximum weight and maximum gross weight.

Mass in Running Order: the weight of a caravan equipped to the manufacturer's standard specification.

Maximum Gross Weight: the maximum allowable total weight set by the manufacturer.

Maximum Technically Permissible Laden Mass (MTPLM): the maximum weight that a trailer chassis can take as stated by the trailer manufacturer. (equals the old GVW)

Unladen Weight: the weight of a vehicle or trailer including its body and any parts normally used with it when working on a road. This does not include the weight of fuel, water or batteries used for moving the vehicle, or the weight of loose equipment or tools.

Licence entitlements for drivers who passed their car licence test after 1/1/1997

Towing vehicle	Licence category	Trailer	Combination	Driving tests required
Vehicles up to 3500kg MAM with up to 8 passenger seats	B	Trailer with a MAM up to 750kg	Maximum combined MAM of 4250kg	Ordinary car driving licence, category B
Vehicles up to 3500kg MAM with up to 8 passenger seats	B	Trailer with MAM greater than 750kg, providing the trailer MAM does not exceed the unladen weight of the towing vehicle	Maximum combined MAM of 3500kg	Ordinary car driving licence, category B
Vehicles up to 3500kg MAM with up to 8 passenger seats	B+E	Trailer over 750kg MAM	No maximum limit on the combined weight for licensing reasons, but see Note 1 below.	Ordinary car driving licence, category B plus practical driving test B+E

Note 1

You should not tow a weight greater than that recommended by the manufacturer of your vehicle (*Highway Code* para 74).
Generally it is recommended that the gross weight of trailers should not exceed 85% of the kerbweight of the towing vehicle.

Entitlements for drivers who passed their car licence test before 1/1/1997

Generally, drivers retain their entitlements to drive a vehicle/trailer combination of up to 8250kg MAM (maximum vehicle weight restricted to 7500kg), and to drive a minibus (buses with 9 to 16 passenger seats, not used for hire or reward) towing a trailer over 750kg MAM. These entitlements (so-called grandfather rights) remain valid until the licence expires. If your licence is re-issued because of a change of address or some other reason, you should check that the new licence includes these rights. If it does not, and you wish to retain them, return your licence to the DVLA and claim all the grandfather rights. Drivers who are banned or disqualified lose their grandfather rights.

Insurance

You must hold or be covered by third party insurance for any vehicles you drive, including trailers. Most insurance policies provide third party cover for your trailer while it is attached to your vehicle, but not all policies do. It is essential that you inform your insurer that you intend to tow a trailer, and check the extent of your cover. Additional cover such as theft or accidental damage to the trailer is usually arranged as an extension to your vehicle policy or through a separate trailer policy.

Most hire companies hold the hirer personally liable for the value of a hired trailer.

Equipment and the law

It is an offence to exceed the plated capacities of a vehicle, trailer or of any safety-critical subcomponents (such as towbars). Exceeding the stated capacities could lead to prosecution under the Plating and Testing or the Construction and Use legislation.

The towing vehicle

The heavier your towing vehicle is in comparison with your trailer, the safer will be your outfit. General safety advice recommends that the laden weight of the trailer should be no more than 85% of the kerbweight of the towing vehicle. With experience, due care and a carefully loaded trailer, this can be increased to a maximum of 100% of the unladen weight, but stability could suffer.

Some commercial and four wheel drive vehicles are designed to tow loads in excess of 100% of their unladen weight. Follow the manufacturer's guidance as to the design of appropriate trailers, the maximum load, and the positioning of the load.

It should be emphasised, however, that even with experience and a fourwheel drive towing vehicle, the standard recommendation is that the maximum laden weight of the trailer should not exceed 85% of the kerbside weight of the towing vehicle. It should never exceed 100%. This may be lower than the weight recommended by the vehicle manufacturer. Manufacturer's recommendations are based on the weight that a vehicle can pull from a standing start on a 12% gradient. Real life towing conditions impose far greater demands on the towing vehicle than this theoretical test. The 85% rule is based on the practical experience of many thousands of towers over many years. It gives the best weight relationship for safe towing. Increasingly, manufacturers are recommending maximum towing limits of less than 85% kerbside weight. Where this is the case, never exceed the manufacturer's recommendations. Otherwise you run the risk of damaging your vehicle.

A loaded trailer should not weigh more than the vehicle manufacturer's recommended maximum towing weight or 85% of the vehicle's kerbside weight, whichever is less.

Vehicles under 1525kg

There is no legal limit placed on the weight of a braked trailer that can be towed by a car or a commercial vehicle under 1525kg unladen weight. Use the manufacturer's plate limit as the legal limit.

Commercial vehicles over 1525kg

Commercially used vehicles with an unladen weight over 1525kg must be fitted with a Ministry Plate under the Goods Vehicle (Plating and Testing) Regulations 1988. The plate gives the MAM and gross train weight for the vehicle.

Manufacturer's recommendations

You should comply with your vehicle manufacturer's recommendations as to the maximum gross weight that you can tow. Most manufacturers recommend a maximum towing weight for each model. This can usually be found on the VIN plate or in the manufacturer's handbook. Type approved vehicles always have the maximum towing weight on their VIN plate. Although this is not a legal maximum, failure to comply with it could be viewed as using a vehicle in an unsafe condition, making you liable to prosecution. It may also invalidate aspects of your insurance.

Mirrors

Mirrors must provide an adequate view to the rear and along both sides of your trailer. If your trailer's size obstructs your rearview mirror, fit additional exterior towing mirrors to improve the view along both sides of your outfit. Mirrors must not project more than 200mm beyond the width of the towing vehicle or the trailer, whichever is wider. Mirrors should be 'e' marked to show that they meet minimum EU standards. When the trailer is not in use, the mirror must not project more than 200mm beyond the sides of your vehicle.

Tachographs

'Any vehicle', with a maximum permissible gross weight MAM over 3500kg 'used for the carriage of goods' must employ a tachograph. Vehicle and trailer combinations exceeding 3500kg combined maximum permissible gross weight MAM, and 'used for the carriage of goods' must also employ a tachograph. Unfortunately what legally constitutes a 'vehicle used for the carriage of goods' is not clear. Case law on the meaning is currently in a state of evolution, so it is not possible to be precise. However, a vehicle which has a maximum gross train weight of less than 3500kg does not require a tachograph even when used with a trailer which takes the combined maximum permissible gross weight over 3500kg, providing the actual gross train weight of the combination remains below 3500kg .

This is because the maximum permissible weight of a combination for tachograph purposes is defined as **whichever is the smaller of:**

● the combined maximum permissable gross weight of vehicle and trailer

or

● the maximum permissable train weight of the towing vehicle.

Added towing mirrors must not project more than 200mm beyond the width of the towing vehicle or the trailer, whichever is wider.

There are numerous exemptions from the requirements of tachograph legislation. Some apply only to the UK, others apply to the whole of the EU.

The Department of Environment, Transport and the Regions produces two leaflets which list these exemptions:

● *Drivers' Hours and Tachograph Rules for Goods Vehicles in the UK and Europe GV262*

● *Drivers' Hours and Tachograph Rules for Passenger Vehicles in the UK and Europe PSV375.*

The leaflets can be obtained from the your local Traffic Area Office. To find the telephone number, look under the entry for the DETR in The Phone Book.

Many 4x4 vehicles and large passenger cars when used for commercial purposes may now fall within the scope of tachograph legislation. If you intend to use a vehicle or vehicle/trailer combination which exceeds 3500kg maximum permissable gross weight MAM to carry goods for commercial purposes; and the vehicle has a maximum permissible gross train weight greater than 3500kg; and you are not covered by any of the exemptions, seek further advice from either the vehicle or trailer manufacturer, the local police or one of the trailer advice organisations listed at the end of the book.

Standard terms applying to key components of the outfit

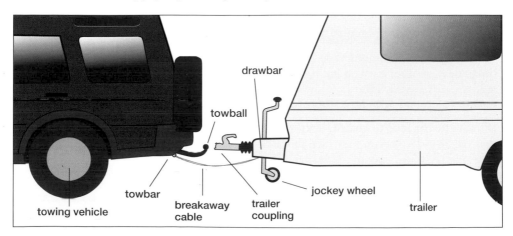

drawbar

towball

towbar

breakaway cable

trailer coupling

jockey wheel

towing vehicle

trailer

Towbars and the law

It is essential to use a correctly fitted towbar, which meets the vehicle manufacturer's specifications. This will ensure that the towbar is strong enough to take any stresses and strains imposed by trailers which meet the vehicle manufacturer's gross trailer weight specification.

Type approval

If you fit a towbar to a car first registered on or after 1 August 1998, you must fit a towbar, that is type approved under Directive 94/20/EC. Failure to do so is an offence under the Construction and Use Regulations 1986. New car models that first came onto the market after 1 January 1996 must only use type approved towbars. The Directive does not require the replacement of towbars legally fitted to vehicles before 1 August 1998, although there may be compelling safety reasons to do so. The Directive requires manufacturers to say whether a model is suitable for towing, how much it can tow, and what its noseweight capacity is. In addition it requires, among other things that towbars:

- attach to all the fixing points provided by the vehicle manufacturer and are designed and tested to carry the loads specified by the manufacturer
- are stamped with an S value – the maximum vertical static load on the towball or eye, measured in kilograms (noseweight)
- are stamped with a D value – calculated from the maximum gross weights of the towing vehicle and trailer and measured in kilonewtons
- do not obscure the number plate when not in use for towing.

Towbars are also required to have a fixture for attaching breakaway or secondary couplings cables.

Failure to comply with type approval

If your towbar fails to comply with the requirements of type approval legislation you may face serious consequences:

- conviction under the terms of the Road Traffic Act 1998 (Construction and Use)
- invalidation of your manufacturer's warranty
- invalidation of your vehicle insurance.

Towballs and other couplings

Towballs and other couplings fitted to light passenger vehicles first registered on or after 1 August 1998 must comply with EC Directive 94/20/EC. This applies to all mechanical couplings whether of the towball, pin/eye, hook/eye or combination type. The Directive covers the size of the couplings; clearances between components of the coupling; and the height of the coupling from the ground when the towing vehicle is laden.

Trailer couplings

Any coupling fitted to a new trailer or sold after 1 January 1999 must also conform to Directive 94/20/EC.

Breakaway and secondary couplings

Towbar manufacturers are advised under BS Code of Practice BSAU 267 to fit towbars with an attachment point for breakaway or secondary couplings cables. Unbraked trailers up to 750kg must be fitted with a secondary coupling method. The secondary coupling should maintain some steering action on the trailer and prevent the nose of the drawbar from touching the ground. Braked trailers up to 3500kg must be fitted with a breakaway cable.

Breakaway cable: A cable connected between the towing vehicle and the trailer's braking mechanism. Designed as a safety device to apply the trailer brakes if the trailer should part from the towing vehicle. After applying the brakes, the cable is designed to break, leaving the trailer detached from the towing vehicle, but unable to freewheel.

Secondary coupling: A cable or chain connected between a trailer and the towing vehicle. Designed to prevent the trailer from becoming detached if the main coupling should fail.

Electrical connections

Towbars are fitted with an international standard seven pin socket (12N) connected to the vehicle's lighting system. Trailers have a corresponding seven pin plug connected to the trailer's lights. It is critically important that both the socket and plug are wired according to international standards, otherwise your lights and indicators may not work correctly. It is advisable to use a system which inactivates your vehicle's rear foglights to avoid the glare caused by foglight reflections off the front of your trailer.

A supplementary seven pin socket (12S) is also available to supply additional circuits used in caravans for interior lights, refrigerators, reversing lights and battery charging.

Some vehicles are now fitted with a new 13 pin socket which combines the functions of both the 12N and 12S sockets. If your trailer has 12N and 12S plugs, either use an adapter cable to connect to the 13 pin socket or get advice on how to wire the trailer cables to a 13 pin plug.

Trailers

Construction of trailers

All light trailers (trailers with a MAM up to 3500kg) are required to comply with the Construction and Use Regulations 1986.

Unbraked trailers

An ordinary category B licence entitles you to tow an unbraked trailer, but whatever your licence entitlements you are only allowed to tow an unbraked trailer with a maximum total weight including load (MAM) of 750kg or half the kerbweight of the towing vehicle, whichever is less. Qualifying agricultural trailers up to 2000kg are exempt. Where a vehicle manufacturer recommends a lower maximum total weight for an unbraked trailer, it is this lower weight that must not be exceeded.

Unbraked trailers must be clearly marked with their year of manufacture, maximum gross weight and their unladen weight. Braked trailers up to 3500kg MAM are not required to display these details when used on UK roads.

Size of trailers

The maximum allowable size of a trailer towed by a car is 7m long and 2.3m wide. The length of a trailer for these calculations excludes the drawbar. Width is measured across the widest fixed points, so includes any mudguards outside the main body of the trailer.

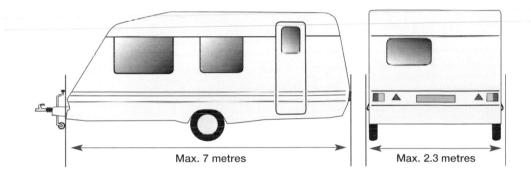

Max. 7 metres   Max. 2.3 metres

Agricultural trailers can be up to 2.55m wide. Four wheeled trailers towed by a qualifying commercial vehicle (MAM greater than 3500kg) can be up to 12m long and 2.55m wide.

Loading

Loads must be secure and not stick out dangerously. Distribute loads as evenly as possible to keep the noseweight within recommended limits.

Manufacturers provide recommendations for the maximum gross weight for their trailers. Most manufacturers include this information on a plate fixed to the trailer. If you exceed this weight you are liable to prosecution. Manufacturers also provide maximum load recommendations for individual wheels and axles, and again these recommendations should be complied with. If individual wheel/axle loads are exceeded, redistribute the load or reduce it.

Projecting loads

The amount by which loads can overhang a trailer is controlled. The permitted maximum overhang beyond the rear of a trailer is 3.05m, and the permitted maximum overhang beyond the sides of a trailer is 305mm each side up to a maximum overall vehicle width of 2.9m. Loads which exceed these permitted limits must be notified to the police.

If the overhang beyond the end of the trailer is between 1 and 2 metres, the end of the overhang must be made clearly visible by attaching a cloth or something similar. If the overhang is between 2 and 3.05 metres, side and end projection marker boards must be fitted. These must be lit at night.

The recommended maximum height for a load is 3m or 1.7 times the wheel track (the distance between wheels on the same axle) of the trailer.

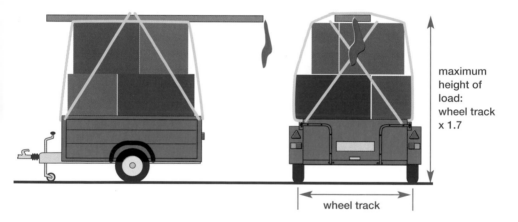

maximum
height of
load:
wheel track
x 1.7

wheel track

Noseweight

It is important to keep the noseweight within the range recommended by the vehicle and trailer manufacturers. Failure to do so will impair the stability of the outfit. Type approved towbars have the maximum noseweight stamped on them – this is given as the S value, the maximum vertical static load measured in kilograms. Recommended noseweights can also be found in your vehicle and trailer manufacturers' handbooks.

Trailer brakes

Trailers over 750kg must have brakes; overrun brakes may be used on trailers up to 3500kg MAM. Where brakes are fitted to a trailer, they must be in working order, whether they are compulsory or not. Since October 1982 trailers which require brakes must comply with EU Directives. These require that:

- brakes must be fitted to all road wheels
- linings must be asbestos free
- the parking brake must operate on at least two wheels
- from October 1982 trailers must be fitted with couplings using a hydraulic damper
- from 1989 only auto-reversing brakes may be fitted.

Spring overrun couplings can still be used as replacement components on trailers manufactured prior to October 1982.

The breakaway cable must be in good condition, and be attached to the towing vehicle whenever the trailer is towed.

Tyres

A trailer must have tyres capable of supporting its maximum permitted axle weight driven at the maximum speed permitted for a trailer. Trailer tyres must comply with the same maintenance regulations as apply to cars and light vans. Tyres must:

- be correctly inflated
- be kept free from certain cuts and other defects
- have at least 1.6mm tread depth across the central three-quarters of the tread face, all the way round the tyre.

Trailers are not required to carry spare wheels, but if spare wheels are used they must also comply with regulations.

Radial and cross-ply combinations

Radial and cross-ply tyres must not be mixed on the same axle of the trailer. You may use a towing vehicle that has legal combination of radial and cross-ply tyres, but you are advised not to because of the effect on stability and control. Best practice is to use the same type of tyre on both vehicle and trailer.

6 ply and 8 ply commercial rated tyres

Mixing of 6 ply and 8 ply tyres on the same axle has become more common as the availablity of 6 ply tyres has declined. Although this is not illegal, the British Rubber Manufacturer's Association advises against mixing tyres of different ply ratings on the same axle.

Bias belted tyres

Some trailer manufacturers are now fitting bias belted tyres. These should not be mixed with either radial or cross-ply tyres on the same trailer. Bias belted tyres can be identified by the use of a dash in the middle of the tyre size designation marking, eg the marking 145–10 identifies a bias belted tyre with a 145mm section width and a 10 inch rim diameter.

Number plate

All trailers must have an approved style number plate carrying the registration number of the towing vehicle. It must be lit at night.

Lights, indicators and triangles

Basically, you should aim to duplicate the standard vehicle rear lights on the end of your trailer and also indicate the physical limits of the load. Lights must be in working order and correctly fitted to the towing vehicle's electrics. Detailed regulations covering trailers can be found in the Road Vehicles Lighting Regulations 1989.

All trailers must have the following lights, indicators and triangles attached to their rear:

- two triangular red reflectors – these warn following drivers that it is a trailer. The triangle does not have to be freestanding, it may be incorporated in a multi-function lamp unit
- two rear red sidelights
- two red stoplights/brakelights
- two amber coloured direction indicator lights, wired to be controlled by the towing vehicle's indicator switch and to flash at the same rate as the vehicle's indicators. Either a warning bleeper or a warning light must be fitted inside the towing vehicle to show the driver that the trailer indicators are working

- number plate light
- trailers greater than 1300mm wide are required to have either one or a maximum of two rear fog lights. The fog lights must be wired through an independent switch and have a device which warns the driver when they are switched on. Vehicles or trailers made before 1 October 1979 are not required to have a rear fog light.

All lights must be visible all the time the trailer is in use on the road. This includes when the trailer is being loaded or unloaded at the kerbside. Any drop tailgates, ramps etc used while loading/unloading must not obscure the lights. If the lights are obscured, a duplicate set fitted above the door opening may be required.

Additional requirements

Depending on the size and weight of the towing vehicle and trailer, the following requirements also apply:

- trailers wider than 1600mm require front reflectors and front marker lights – front marker lights are not required by trailers less than 2300m long made before October 1985, or immersible boat trailers
- trailers wider than 2.1m, made after October 1991, must have front and rear end outline markers
- trailers longer than 6m, made after 1 October 1990, must have side marker lights – but not immersible boat trailers
- trailers longer than 5m must have amber side reflectors
- drivers of towing vehicles with a gross weight over 7500kg are advised to fit rear marker plates to trailers below 3500kg.

Any marker boards used to mark projecting loads must also be lit at night.

Regulations governing specific types of trailer

In addition to the general regulations, there may be additional regulations controlling the use of trailers used for specific purposes. Examples of these are the Welfare of Animals (Transport) Order 1997, regulating the carrying of livestock, or the Health and Safety at Work legislation and the EC Directives controlling the use of winches on vehicle and boat transporters. The manufacturers of specialist trailers are a good source of information on these specific regulations.

Traffic law

There are specific regulations applying to trailers and vehicles towing trailers.

- Unless a lower limit applies, cars, car derived vans and motorcycles towing trailers must not exceed 60mph on a motorway or dual carriageway, or 50mph on a single carriageway. These are maximum permitted speeds and may often be too fast for the circumstances.

- Vehicles towing a trailer must not use the right-hand lane of a motorway with three or more lanes, unless signs indicate otherwise or the nearside lanes are blocked by roadworks.

- Trailers must not be left on a road at night without lights.

- A trailer must not be left on a road so as to cause an obstruction.

- A trailer must not be left on the road by itself unless the brake is on or at least one wheel is effectively prevented from moving.

- You must not tow more than your licence permits, nor overload your trailer. You should not tow anything heavier than the vehicle manufacturer recommends.

- You must secure your load. It must not stick out dangerously.

- Distribute the load evenly throughout the trailer.

- You should not tow a passenger in a trailer (including caravans). There is an exception – passengers in a broken down vehicle may be towed at not more than 30mph providing both vehicles are connected by a rigid towbar.

- If you are driving a large or slow moving vehicle do not hold up a long queue of traffic. Pull in where it is safe and let the traffic pass.

- Vehicles with trailers are not allowed to use parking meter zones.

Towing broken down cars

When towed, a broken down car is classed as an unbraked trailer, even if towed on a braked dolly. The maximum gross vehicle weight for an unbraked trailer is 750kg. Apart from a handful of models, nearly all cars have a GVW of more than 750kg. Therefore towing a car by either rope or dolly for any other reason than removing it to a local garage or place of safety is illegal. The only legal option is to use a car transporter.

Ropes or chains

Where a rope or chain is used to tow a trailer, the distance between the towing vehicle and the trailer must not be greater than 4.5m. If it is greater than 1.5m, a bright coloured rag or a piece of luminous material must be tied to the rope to warn other road users. The same requirements apply when ropes or chains are used to tow cars.

Chapter 2

Putting together a safe outfit – built-in stability

A well-matched outfit

This chapter is about inbuilt safety – putting together an outfit which is inherently safe. The key to this is matching the towing vehicle to trailer and load. The towing vehicle must be heavy and powerful enough to pull the load safely. The trailer must be strong enough to take the load you wish to transport. The loads placed on both vehicle and trailer must be within their manufacturer's specifications. A well-matched outfit will be stable and safe to drive. A mismatched outfit will be difficult to drive, unstable and possibly illegal.

The towing vehicle

The heavier your towing vehicle compared with your trailer, the more stable will be your outfit. The best combination is the heaviest towing vehicle with the lightest trailer that will do the job. The more powerful your towing vehicle the easier it is to maintain speed, negotiate hazards and accelerate out of dangerous situations. Besides weight and performance the other factors which affect a vehicle's ability to tow are its height, centre of gravity, suspension, wheelbase and wheel track.

Power steering is a definite advantage, especially when reversing. Good brakes are essential given the extra load, with a preference for disc brakes all round. Anti-lock braking systems (ABS) have been shown in practical trials to considerably reduce braking distances when towing. Four wheel drive vehicles are generally able to tow heavier loads than two wheel drive vehicles and are better at maintaining traction in difficult conditions.

Weight

The recommended weight for a towing vehicle depends on the weight that it is required to tow – the heavier the loaded trailer the heavier the towing vehicle needs to be. The standard recommendation is:

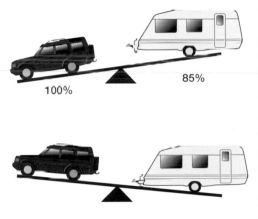

100%   85%

A loaded trailer should not weigh more than the vehicle manufacturer's recommended maximum towing weight or 85% of the vehicle's kerbweight, whichever is less.

If your trailer is heavier than the towing vehicle you run the risk of 'the tail wagging the dog'. On hills the trailer may start to pull or push the towing vehicle, causing the driver to lose control. On the level, you risk the trailer developing a potentially disastrous pendulum action called snaking.

Both the maximum towing weight and the kerbweight of a vehicle are usually given in the manufacturer's handbook. To work out 85% of the kerbweight complete the following calculation:

Kerbweight (from manufacturer's handbook) ÷ **100 x 85 = Answer**

eg Take for example a typical mid-range saloon, which we shall call the Chevin 1.7 GLS. The Chevin's handbook gives its kerbweight as **1215kg**

1215 ÷ 100	= 12.15
12.15 x 85	= 1032.75
85% of the Chevin's kerbweight	= 1032.75 kg

However, the Chevin's handbook also says that the maximum weight that this particular model should tow is 1000kg. It is this lower weight, rather than the 1032.75kg given by the 85% rule, which provides the safe maximum towing limit for this vehicle.

Wheelbase and wheeltrack

The bigger the footprint of a towing vehicle the more stable it will be. The longer its wheelbase (the distance between the front and back wheels) and the wider its wheeltrack (the distance between the nearside and offside wheels) the better it will be for towing.

Performance

Different engines produce maximum torque (turning force) and maximum power (the maximum work an engine is capable of doing) at different engine revs. A good tow vehicle requires a good torque-spread rather than massive power at high revs. The most satisfactory towing engines develop a good amount of torque at low engine speeds and sustain it over a wide range. This provides flexibility at all speeds. Diesel engines generally produce less power than the same sized petrol engines, but because they produce plenty of torque at low revs, they often make better towing vehicles. This is particularly so with turbodiesels, which typically produce maximum torque at around 2800 revs compared with 4600 revs for some petrol engines.

Gears

Gearboxes are said to be high geared or low geared. High gearing means that fewer revolutions of an engine are needed for each revolution of the wheels. Low gearing means that more revolutions of the engine are needed for each revolution of the wheels.

Low geared engines produce greater turning power at the wheels because each revolution of the wheels represents the added-up turning power of a greater number of engine revolutions. High geared engines turn the wheels faster because they require fewer engine revolutions for each turn of the wheels.

The best towing vehicle is one with low overall gearing because of its greater wheel turning power at low engine speeds. This reduces the need to be constantly dropping down gears when climbing hills, and so saves fuel and driver fatigue. The low gearing reduces the top road speed of the vehicle, but this is not usually a problem when towing because speed limits and the need for stability already restrict top speeds.

Five or more speed gearboxes

Five or more speed gearboxes are generally better for towing than four speed boxes because the extra gears reduce the range that each gear is required to cover. This allows the lower gears to start at a lower gearing ratio than would otherwise be the case. The fifth and higher gears are rarely used when towing.

Estate cars

Estates are often fitted with lower gearing than other versions in the same range. Despite their sometimes extensive rear overhangs (the distance between the centre of the rear axle and the towball – the shorter the overhang the better the stability), estates are often chosen as tow vehicles. Generally, owners consider that their low gear ratio, firmer suspension and good storage space makes up for what they might lack in stability.

Automatic transmissions

Automatic transmissions generally perform as well, if not better, than manual gearboxes for towing purposes. Their maximum torque at minimum revs is particularly helpful on hill starts. In particular, modern low-ratio automatic gearboxes improve climbing performance on hills and engine braking on descents.

Oil coolers

The extra load of a trailer will cause the temperature of the transmission oil in an automatic gearbox to rise. The hotter the oil the shorter the life of the gearbox. If the oil seriously overheats, which it might do with a heavy load or hot weather or high speeds, the gearbox can fail in a matter of miles. You can avoid the inconvenience and considerable expense of repairing the gearbox by fitting an additional oil cooling unit. Manufacturers' claims as to the towing capabilities of automatic transmissions should be viewed with great caution. The general advice is to fit an additional oil cooler if you have automatic transmission.

Suspension

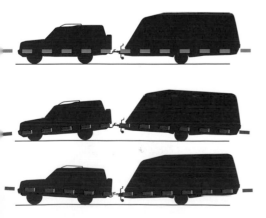

The trailer's noseweight weighs primarily on the rear suspension of the towing vehicle. It is important for the stability of the outfit that it remains more or less level, under this loading. If the rear of the vehicle sags excessively, several problems can arise – handling will be compromised, the headlights will be tilted too high and ground clearance can become inadequate. Reducing the noseweight will not solve the problem because reducing noseweight below recommended levels will endanger the stability of the outfit.

Vehicles fitted with self-levelling suspensions will usually be able to make the necessary adjustments to compensate for the additional load. With other vehicles, make sure that you have not overloaded the rear of the vehicle before the trailer is attached. If the loading in the vehicle is moderate and the rear still sags excessively under the recommended noseweight, have the vehicle's suspension and shock absorbers checked. If the suspension and shock absorbers are defective they should be replaced, but first seek the manufacturer's advice on whether it would be advisable to upgrade them.

Suspension aids

If the suspension is performing correctly, but still sags excessively under the noseweight, additional aids can be fitted to stiffen it. There are different aids to suit the different types of suspension but broadly they fall into two groups: aids which replace the shock absorbers and aids which supplement the existing suspension.

Vehicles are designed so that their suspensions and shock absorbers are compatible. If one of these components is stiffened on its own, the other may no longer be able to perform satisfactorily. It is safest to upgrade suspension and shock absorbers together to maintain compatibility.

Altering a vehicle's suspension for towing purposes will alter its ride and handling characteristics when driven solo. If the rear suspension is upgraded and the front suspension is not, the stability of the vehicle when driven on its own may be adversely affected. Before making these alterations get competent advice – from the vehicle or aid manufacturer, a towing organisation or a competent auto-engineer.

Overhang

The load placed on the towing vehicle's suspension by a trailer is affected by the length of the vehicle's rear overhang (the distance between the centre of the rear axle and the towball) and the height of the tow hitch. The longer the overhang and the higher the tow hitch, the greater the load on the rear suspension. A short rear overhang and a tow hitch which is level with the coupling on the trailer is best.

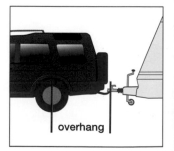

overhang

Height

The position of the tow-hitch affects the stresses imposed on the towing vehicle and the trailer. The British and European standard height for hitch points is, with the vehicle conventionally laden (= occupant plus luggage for each available seat), between 350mm and 420mm above ground. Not all vehicles comply with this standard.

If the vehicle's hitch point is too high, there is a risk that the rear of the trailer will hit the ground when travelling over uneven surfaces such as speed humps.

If the trailer is double axled and has independent suspension on each axle, a vehicle tow hitch which is too high will lift the trailer's front set of wheels and place an excessive burden on the rear set. The trailer will tend to see-saw on the rear set of wheels, imposing excessive wear and strains on the towbar, drawbar and all the other coupling components. It will also overload the vehicle's rear suspension and reduce braking and steering control at the front wheels.

If the hitch point is too low, there is a risk that the jockey wheel will ground and send shock waves through the coupling mechanism. Double axled, independently suspended trailers will tend to see-saw and put additional strains on the coupling components.

Using a drop plate to lower a hitch point which is too high is not a trouble-free solution. Firstly a drop plate imposes an additional set of stresses and strains on the towbar and chassis which may be beyond their design limits. Secondly, introducing a drop plate on a type approved vehicle is not permissible unless the drop plate itself is also type approved. Again it is worth seeking advice from the vehicle or towbar manufacturer.

Tyres

The tyres of the towing vehicle have a considerable influence on the stability of the outfit. Tyres should be in good condition and correctly inflated. Where the manufacturer gives different pressures for high and low loadings of the vehicle, use the high pressure recommendations for towing. If the manufacturer does not recommend a different pressure for high loads, increase the rear tyre pressure by 4 to 7 psi (0.3 to 0.5 bar).

It is particularly important that tyres are correctly inflated when towing. Low and uneven tyre pressures reduce stability and can lead to tyre failure.

Tyre type

You are recommended to fit the same type of tyre – cross-ply or radial – to all wheels of the outfit, towing vehicle and trailer. This provides the best stability. It is legal, although not recommended, to have:

- radials on your towing vehicle and cross-ply tyres on your trailer
- cross-plys on your vehicle and radials on your trailer
- cross-plys on the front and radials on the rear of your vehicle and either all radials or all cross- plys on your trailer.

Trailer tyres

Radial and cross-ply

All the tyres on the trailer should be either cross-ply or radial; they must not be mixed. They should also be of the same size, ply rating and load/speed characteristics. When replacing cross-ply tyres with radials, it is important to check that the load capacity of the replacement tyres is adequate. Radials may have lower load capacity than the same sized cross-plys. Although it is not required in law, it is good practice to carry a spare for your trailer. The spare on your towing vehicle will almost certainly be of the wrong size and specification for your trailer. Your trailer spare must be of the same type as the other tyres on the trailer. All tyres must be correctly inflated and in good condition. Tyres that are unevenly or incorrectly inflated will reduce the stability of the trailer.

Speed and weight limits

Like other tyres, trailer tyres are rated for their maximum speed and load; these ratings are moulded on the sidewall of the tyre as a service description code. The code consists of a load index and a speed symbol. The service description code is located near to the size designation code on the wall of the tyre. The tables below provide a key to the code. Do not exceed these limits by overloading the trailer or driving too fast. You will also find tyre markings which state the 'max load' and 'max pressure'. These are American and Canadian markings and do not apply to the UK and Europe.

Tyre load indices	Load index	Load kg	Load index	Load kg	Load index	Load kg
	60	250	82	475	104	900
	61	257	83	487	105	925
	62	265	84	500	106	950
	63	272	85	515	107	975
	64	280	86	530	108	1000
	65	290	87	545	109	1030
	66	300	88	560	110	1060
	67	307	89	580	111	1090
	68	315	90	600	112	1120
	69	325	91	615	113	1150
	70	335	92	630	114	1180
	71	345	93	650	115	1215
	72	355	94	670	116	1250
	73	365	95	690	117	1285
	74	375	96	710	118	1320
	75	387	97	730	119	1360
	76	400	98	750	120	1400
	77	412	99	775	121	1450
	78	425	100	800	122	1500
	79	437	101	825	123	1550
	80	450	102	850	124	1600
	81	462	103	875	125	1650

Speed symbol table	Speed Symbol	Maximum mph for tyre
	L	75
	M	81
	N	87
	P	93
	Q	100
	R	106
	S	113
	T	118
	U	124
	H	130
	V	150
	W	168
	Y	186

For example a tyre with service description 84T is suitable for a maximum load on that tyre of 500kg at a maximum speed of 118mph.

When towing items with an uneven weight distribution, it is important that the individual maximum axle loads are not exceeded. Uneven bulging of the trailer tyres would suggest that either the load needs re-positioning or that axle loads need checking on a weighbridge. The load and speed marking of a tyre is marked on its side.

Use of trailers in countries with higher speed limits

In the past many UK trailer manufacturers have made use of a concession called 'bonus load'. This allows manufacturers to uprate the load bearing capacity of tyres providing the maximum speed at which they are used is limited to 62mph (100km/h). This presents no problems for towing in the UK, so long as the specified maximum load and the maximum speed limit of 60mph are observed. But if trailers with bonus loaded tyres are used in countries with higher speed limits, problems could arise. If these tyres are used at full load at speeds greater than 100km/h their design specification will be exceeded, creating a risk of tyre failure.

Before using trailers abroad at speeds greater than 100km/h, check with the trailer manufacturer whether bonus loads have been used to calculate the maximum permitted axle loads. If they have, keep your speeds below 100km/h. Trailer manufacturers now recognise that this is a problem and are increasingly fitting larger tyres rated at their standard load capacities. France and some other countries require trailers to be only fitted with tyres that are suitable for use at the maximum speed limit.

Older trailers may be fitted with cross-ply tyres which are no longer available. When one of these tyres needs to be replaced you should replace all the tyres on the trailer with radials, not forgetting the spare if you have one. Tubeless radial tyres can only be fitted to wheels with safety rims. Many older trailers do not have these rims, and the usual replacement solution is to fit radial tyres with tubes. Before doing this you should check with the tyre manufacturer because not all radial tyres are suitable for use with tubes.

Tyre ageing and cracking

Tyres that stand stationary for long periods of time age and crack more quickly than those in regular use. As a result of the prolonged load, the tyre wall tends to weaken in one particular spot. Many trailers such as caravans and boat trailers stand unused throughout the winter. If you know this is going to happen it is advisable to shield the tyres from direct sunlight and to lift the weight off the tyres. Before you do this, consult your trailer manual or manufacturer for advice on appropriate jacking and support points and the types of support to use. Do not support your trailer on piles of bricks.

Before re-using the trailer the following season check for any cracking or deformation in the tyres; if you have any concerns get specialist advice. Because of infrequent use and a good depth of tread, trailer tyres may appear to be in good condition when they are not. Inspect trailer tyres regularly – running your hand over the tyre surface can usually detect bulges better than your eyes – and discard them after five or, at the most, seven years. There are indications that commercial grade tyres (with a C suffix), age more quickly, and that their service life may be as little as three years.

Couplings

All the components of the coupling between the towing vehicle and the trailer must be capable of taking the actual load of the trailer and comply with any statutory requirements. You should regularly check that they are in good condition.

Towbar

See Chapter 1

A quality towbar designed to cope with the maximum load that you will place upon it and which also meets the required standards is essential. Since 1 August 1998 all towbars fitted to new vehicles must be type approved. Towbars fitted to vehicles registered before this date should still be fitted to the vehicle manufacturer's specifications, and tested to BS 114b. Failure to use all the manufacturer's fixing points is likely to:

● reduce safety when towing

● unduly stress the body or chassis of the towing vehicle

● invalidate your vehicle manufacturer's warranty.

It is important to check regularly that the bolts attaching the towbar to the vehicle remain at their specified torque settings and that there is no metal failure or rusting around the fixing points.

Hitches

There are several types of hitch which may be fitted to the towbar – two types of towball, a variety of towing eyes plus combination hitches. Whatever you use it is essential that the trailer and the vehicle components are compatible.

Towballs

The standard towball in the UK and Europe is the 50mm towball. Couplings designed to fit the 50mm ball are not compatible with the old UK standard and current US 2 inch (2") towballs. It is dangerous to mix 50mm and 2" towballs and couplings, whichever way round.

Unless you are using an inhead friction type stabiliser that attaches to your towball, you should ensure that there is a thin coat of grease on the towball to reduce friction and minimise wear. If the coupling rattles on the ball, it may need replacing. There is currently no clear regulatory guidance on tolerances for towball diameters. Manufacturers recommend replacement of the towball if its diameter falls below 49.61mm. Protect the towball with a cover when it is not in use.

When a trailer is not attached, your towball must not obscure the number plate. If it does you are liable to an on the spot fine.

Coupling heads

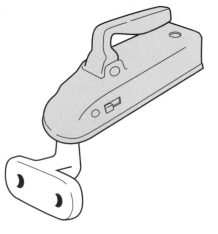

Coupling heads are designed to accommodate towballs down to 49mm in size. Most heads have wear indicators or wear adjusters built into their design. All heads have a locking device to lock the head onto the towball. On some heads the locking device is automatic, on others the locking handle has to be manually engaged. Some heads also incorporate an indicator button to show when the head is safely locked on the ball.

All parts of the coupling head and its locking and indicator mechanisms must be well maintained and in good working order. Regularly clean the grime out of the inside of the coupling head with a cloth dampened with white spirit, and relubricate with a thin layer of grease. If the wear indicator or take-up in

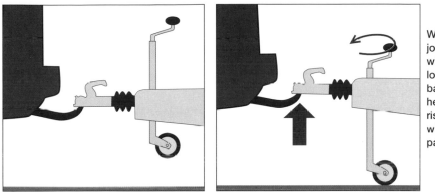

When the jockey wheel is fully lowered, the ball and head should rise together without parting.

the wear adjuster indicate that excessive wear has taken place, check both the ball and coupling head for wear. It is generally recommended that both ball and head are replaced at the same time, because this increases their service life.

If your trailer has a jockey wheel it is good practice to use the jockey wheel to check that the ball and head are securely connected. Wind down the jockey wheel until the ball and head rise without parting. This indicates that the head is correctly locked onto the ball. Do not overdo it though – you might damage the jockey wheel and/or drawbar.

Towing eyes

There are several types of towing eye in use: in the UK 30 and 40mm diameter eyes are the most common for private and commercial use and 50mm for agricultural use. There is also a 76mm NATO size which is standard for military and heavy commercial use. Generally towballs are preferred for private use because they are much quieter than towing eyes and jaws.

Do not mix UK and DIN fittings

DIN eyes with similar sizes to UK sizes are commonly used in Europe. DIN eyes have a hardened steel insert and must not be used with UK jaws. The hardened steel insert cuts into standard UK pins.

Eyes are designed to tow on the pin and brake and corner on the jaw. There should be sufficient clearance to allow free vertical and horizontal movement. This is achieved by having an eye diameter bigger than the pin diameter, providing a sufficient gap to allow the outside of the eye to contact the back of the jaws on braking and cornering. The top and bottom jaws are splayed to allow vertical movement. The recommended clearance for eye movement between the pin and jaw is approximately 3mm. This allows free movement but avoids excessive rattle. Do not use parallel jaws because they prevent adequate vertical movement. They cause strain on all the components of the coupling and are dangerous.

Guidelines for the safe use of towing eyes

Make sure that:

● DIN eyes are not fitted to standard UK jaws

● eyes and jaw are of compatible sizes so that the eye tows on the pin and brakes on the jaw

● neither eye nor pin is worn. If the eye rides on the pin under braking and cornering it will tend to bend and jam.

Towball/jaw combinations

Combination towball/jaws are versatile because they allow trailers with different types of hitch to be towed. There are a number of different types available. One type has a fixed 50mm ball attached to the upper jaw, and a separate removable towpin secured by a clip. Another type also has a fixed ball on the upper jaw, but has a non-removable articulating hook arrangement. Additionally there is a type which has a 50mm ball as an integral part of the towpin. This type has several variants, some of which, depending on their locking mechanism, raise important safety issues. The safe type uses primary and secondary locking features for failsafe reasons. The less safe type uses only a single clip to secure the pin in the jaw. If the clip should fail, or the driver neglect to insert it properly the clip could dislodge and release the trailer. It is best to ensure that components are approved to Directive EC94/20 which tests the design and integrity of manufacture for safety and reliability in operation.

Towbar adaptors

There are various adaptors which allow you to attach other items besides trailers to your tow hitch. These are of two types: those that allow you to attach additional items when towing a trailer and those which can only attach to the tow hitch when no trailer is being towed.

Adaptors which allow you to attach items, such as cycles, in addition to the trailer need to be used with caution. The weight of the item carried must be added to that of the trailer noseweight to arrive at the total noseweight loading for the hitch. This must remain within the maximum limits set by the vehicle and towbar manufacturers. Reducing the noseweight of the trailer to remain within the limits is not an acceptable solution because it would destabilise the trailer.

Adaptors which attach to the tow hitch itself prevent this particular problem arising. The load must still remain within the manufacturers' noseweight limits – a couple of bikes could easily exceed 70kg. You should also ensure that the load does not obscure the vehicle light-clusters and the number plate. When this cannot be done, for example with some towbar cycle racks, you must place a lighting board at the back of the bikes.

Towbar adaptors on type approved vehicles

On a type approved vehicle, no adaptors may be fitted between the towbar and the towball unless allowance for an adaptor was included in the type approval for the towbar. If you wish to fit a stabiliser or other adaptor to a type approved towbar you must find out from the manufacturer whether it complies with the type approval specification for that towbar. If the towbar is not approved for the use of an adaptor, the use of an adaptor would be illegal. Always check with the manufacturer befor altering a type approved towbar in any way.

Noseweight

See also Chapter 3, Noseweight

Noseweight is the downward pressure on the tow hitch exerted by the trailer. Having the correct noseweight is critical for trailer stability. Your trailer should ride level or slightly nose down. If the noseweight is too light the trailer will bounce around, and the likelihood of snaking is greatly increased. If the noseweight is too heavy, excessive strain will be placed on the vehicle's rear suspension and on the coupling components of both vehicle and trailer. The towing vehicle will be destabilised, its headlights will tilt upwards and the couplings may fail.

The usual recommended noseweight range is between 50 and 100 kilograms, but you should check the maximum noseweight capacity of your vehicle in the manufacturer's handbook. Never exceed this figure. Your trailer manufacturer may also provide a recommended noseweight. Ideally, the recommended vehicle and trailer noseweights should match. Where there is a discrepancy you should use the lower of the two figures.

The noseweight exerted by a trailer depends on how the trailer is loaded. By moving the load or parts of the load forward of the trailer wheels, you will increase noseweight; moving the load or part of it behind the wheels will reduce it. Arrange the load of your trailer to achieve the recommended noseweight, but avoid placing excessive weight to the rear of the trailer because it will cause instability.

Measuring the noseweight

The only way to be sure of the noseweight is to measure it. You can buy a purpose-made device to do this or do what most people do – use a set of bathroom scales.

Cut a piece of wood (a piece of broom-handle works well) so that when it is placed between the bathroom scales and the coupling head the head is level at the same height as the vehicle hitch point. Make allowance for the thickness of any wood placed on the scales to spread the load. Load the trailer and make sure the brakes are on. Put the scales under the coupling head. Raise the drawbar either by hand or using the jockey wheel. Weigh the noseweight by resting the trailer load on the stick between the coupling head and scales. Make sure that no weight remains on the jockey wheel by raising it clear of the ground, and that any steadies on a caravan are raised. Adjust the position of the load and reweigh until the desired noseweight is achieved.

Weighing the noseweight by placing the jockey wheel on the scales will give an inaccurate reading.

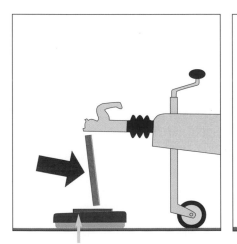
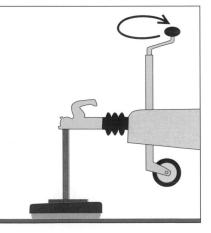

Bathroom scales

Achieving the optimum noseweight

The noseweight should never exceed the limits set by the vehicle and trailer manufacturers, but within these limits it is worth cautiously experimenting to find the optimum weight for your combination. Under actual driving conditions the static noseweight is altered by the effect of the airstream on the outfit. This effect depends on the specific aerodynamics of the trailer and load being towed; with some caravans it tends to lift the nose. The effect on open trailers will vary with the load carried.

Breakaway cables and secondary couplings

Unbraked trailers up to 750kg must be fitted with a secondary coupling which will keep the trailer attached to the towing vehicle if the primary coupling fails. Braked trailers up to 3500kg must be fitted with a breakaway cable which, in the event of primary coupling failure, will apply the trailer's brakes and then snap. You are not allowed to tow a trailer without attaching one or other of these cables to the towing vehicle. So it is important for legal and safety reasons to build the attachment of the breakaway/secondary coupling cable into your hitching routine.

The breakaway cable operates by pulling on the handbrake. It will only apply the handbrake if the breakaway cable pulls directly to the front of the handbrake. This can be ensured by passing the breakaway cable through a lug fitted to the front of the drawbar.

New towbars are required to have an attachment point for breakaway or secondary couplings cables but older towbars may not have such a point. Where there is none, do not attach the cable to a weak vehicle part, such as the bumper, because it will probably break away before doing its job. If the cable cannot be secured to part of the towbar, you are permitted to loop it around the stem of the towball but this is not advisable because it could easily slip off. It is better to fit an accessory such as a pigtail to the towbar onto which you can attach the cable.

Cables must not drag on the ground and should be kept in good condition. Check them regularly and replace if there is any evidence of fraying, kinking or splitting. Breakaway cables are matched to the particular braking system on the trailer and are designed to snap when those brakes are fully applied. It is therefore important to replace a defective cable with the correct part or it may not work properly.

The braking system

Overrun brakes

Current braking systems on trailers between 750kg and 3500kg are hydraulically damped, auto-reverse, overrun systems. On these trailers the coupling head is mounted on a shaft which moves inside a tube attached to the frame of the trailer. When the shaft slides along the tube it pushes a lever which applies the brakes. Whilst towing, the shaft is normally at full extent, but when the towing vehicle brakes, the momentum of the trailer forces the shaft along the tube and operates the trailer brakes.

Hydraulic damping

Since October 1982 these overrun braking mechanisms are required to be hydraulically damped to smooth short sharp movements. This prevents the brakes coming on at every small reduction in speed, and produces a smoother ride. Overrun mechanisms without hydraulic damping are called spring overrun couplings and are still legal on pre-1982 trailers.

See the section later in this chapter on old trailers and new vehicles.

Auto-reverse brakes

Auto-reverse mechanisms allow the trailer to be reversed without the brakes being applied by the overrun system. Trailers made after 1989 are required to have auto-reversing brakes. Older brake systems had a lever to manually disable the brakes for reversing, reducing the manoeuvrability of the outfit and running the risk of leaving the brakes disabled through forgetfulness.

The handbrake

The handbrake is interconnected with the overrun braking mechanism but can apply the brakes independently. It is used to apply the brakes for parking and should be fully engaged before uncoupling the trailer from the towing vehicle.

The handbrake has to apply braking in the reverse as well as the forward direction, for parking on backward slopes etc. To do this it operates a complex mechanism in the wheel hub brake assembly. This mechanism will only work correctly if the brakes and all the linkages are correctly adjusted. It is essential when making these adjustments to start at the brake back plate on the wheel hub and work forwards towards the coupling. If you try to compensate for a decline in braking by only adjusting the brake rod length, you may improve the road braking but you will weaken the reverse parking brake. The next time you park facing uphill, your trailer will run down hill as soon as you unhitch it.

After reversing, the brakes are disengaged by the auto-reverse mechanism. Always drive forward a little to re-set the brakes in their normal position.

Even when your braking system is well adjusted it is always a good idea to put chocks under your wheels when you park on a slope.

A safe braking system

The braking system on a trailer is complex. It requires fine adjustment and regular maintenance. Unless you are completely sure about what you are doing, leave work on the braking system to specialists. Your safety and that of other road users depends on your brakes being in good working order. Get into the habit of routine inspection and maintenance:

- visually inspect the brake system and check the coupling every time you hitch the trailer
- lubricate coupling and the brake linkages every three months or 2000 miles. Do not gun grease into the brake bowden cables under any circumstances
- reset the brake shoes and all the brake linkages every 3000 miles – replace brake shoes with warranted parts when their linings reach 2mm thickness.

After adjusting the brakes take the trailer for a road test. Feel the brake drums to see if they are hot. If they are, the brakes need readjusting.

Checking the coupling

Check the coupling every time you hitch the trailer.

- Check the rubber bellows – if they are damaged, perished or badly fitting replace them – if any road dirt gets into the drawbar bearings it will damage them.

- Grasp the coupling head and move it up and down – if there is free movement the bearings which support the drawtube are worn and need replacing.

- Chock the wheels and release the handbrake. Push the coupling head towards the back of the trailer. If it fails to move or goes back without resistance the damper is worn and must be replaced.

Coupling and trailer brake components are precisely matched. It is important to use compatible parts when replacing worn components. The major cause of coupling damper failure is poor or irregular brake adjustment.

Signs that the trailer brakes need attention

- Banging or snatching during braking – suggests a worn coupling damper

- jerking when braking

- poor braking

- weak resistance at upper end of trailer handbrake movement

- overheating of brake drums/wheel hubs.

If you experience any of these symptoms, get your braking system checked immediately.

Old trailers and new vehicles

The speed capabilities of roads and vehicles have increased enormously over the last 30 or 40 years. The brake systems on modern trailers have been improved to accommodate increases in speed. But there are still many older trailers, legally on the road, which have brake systems designed for a slower age. If you put one of these trailers behind a modern vehicle and tow at current maximum speeds you risk having a serious accident. Tow older trailers at a speed appropriate to their specifications. These speeds should be low enough to ensure that the outfit remains fully stable under normal progress, cornering and braking.

Electrical fittings

The trailer's electrical components – the trailer lights, indicators etc – are powered by the towing vehicle whilst in transit. Power is supplied through a connector, the socket side of which is wired to the tow vehicle and the plug side to the trailer. On hitching, the trailer is plugged into the vehicle socket, connecting the trailer circuits to the vehicle circuits.

Most vehicles do not come with a trailer connector socket as a standard fitting. The socket has to be fitted later, usually at the same time as the towbar. Electrical systems vary considerably between vehicles, and wiring the socket to the vehicle's electrics is a specialist job. If you do not know precisely what you are doing, you could easily damage the vehicle's electrical components, invalidate your warranty and create a fire risk. Before connecting the socket to the vehicle's electrics either get advice from the vehicle manufacturer or a specialist supplier. Alternatively have a specialist do the work.

The standard electrical fitting is a seven pin 12N connector, which is usually coloured black. The socket part of the connector is wired to the vehicle electrics and the plug part to trailer road lights. The terminals on both sides of the connector must be correctly wired or the trailer lights will malfunction. The terminal connections are set out in the table below.

Terminal	Colour	Function
1	yellow	nearside indicator
2	blue	rear fog light(s)
3	white	common return (earth)
4	green	offside indicator
5	brown	offside tail and front marker light
6	red	brake lights
7	black	nearside tail and front marker light, number plate light

It has been found that trailer metalwork does not provide a reliable electrical return connection. Only use the number 3 pin and white wire connections for earth returns. Equally it is essential that there is a good pin 3 earth connection from the towing vehicle's 12N socket to the vehicle bodywork. All connections to the vehicle electrical system should be properly made with the appropriate connectors. Twisted wire connections covered by tape make poor, unsafe connections. If your vehicle has computer controlled electronics, do not splice trailer connections into the loom because it may damage the computer. Get advice from the vehicle manufacturer. All cables should be attached to the bodywork with ties or tape to protect them from physical damage and excessive vibration.

12S Caravan connector

Another standard seven pin connector, the 12S, usually coloured grey or white, provides an electrical connection specifically for caravans. Its pins supply power from the vehicle to the caravan for the reversing lights, battery charging, the interior lights, the fridge and two spares; it also has an earth pin. 12N and 12S connectors have different pin configurations and will not fit each other.

1999 modification to 12S wiring

The wiring specification for 12S caravan connectors changed from the 1999 model year (from 1 September 1998 onwards). The wiring on vehicles has yet to catch up with this change. It is likely that even with new vehicles you will need to modify the vehicle wiring to ensure that the new 12S connector works properly. Altering the wiring on a new vehicle may invalidate its warranty. The best advice is to resolve the compatibility and warranty issues with your supplier before buying.

12N and 12S mountings

The towing vehicle's connectors are usually fixed onto a mounting plate beside the towball. The method of attaching some types of stabiliser prevents connectors being mounted on the same side of the towball as the stabiliser. If this is the case, the best side for the stabiliser should be decided first and the connector(s) fitted on the other side. If 12N and 12S connectors are to be fitted one above the other, care should be taken that the lower one cannot hit the ground. It is also advisable to keep the connectors at least 150mm away from the exhaust.

There is also a European standard 13 pin connector which combines the functions of the 12N and 12S connectors. Adaptors are available to convert 13 pin European connectors to 12N and 12S British connectors.

Vehicle indicator units

The indicator flasher units in many private vehicles are not designed to run the trailer indicators as well. When trailer indicators are wired into them they fail to meet legal performance standards. The vehicle's relay unit must either be replaced with a bigger one or the trailer's indicators powered independently. Whichever solution is adopted the vehicle and trailer indicators must flash in unison and at the legal rate.

Stabilisers

Stabilisers can help to improve the stability of an outfit by increasing the friction at the joint between the vehicle and the trailer – the hitch point. This reduces snaking (left–right) movements of the trailer, and some stabilisers reduce pitching (up–down) movements as well. You should not fit a stabiliser in an attempt to cure an inherently unstable combination. First make sure that you have a well-matched outfit with the correct noseweight and an appropriately laden trailer. Then consider the need for a stabiliser. If you fit a stabiliser to an inherently unstable combination you merely raise the speed at which instability occurs, thereby increasing the seriousness of any resulting accident.

Stabilisers are of greatest benefit to high-sided trailers such as caravans which are subject to wind-buffeting from large vehicles and sudden wind gusts.

Points to watch

● Inhead stabilisers that couple onto the towball require the towball to be totally grease-free. Before coupling, check that the towball has not been contaminated by grease from other trailers.

● Some stabilisers require a longer neck on the towball to achieve a 250 pivot, up and down. If you hitch a trailer with one of these stabilisers to a standard towball you risk damaging the trailer's overrun assembly on the towball shoulders and the vehicle bumper.

● Some pitch-controlling stabilisers have a load equalising effect, which shifts some of the load from the coupling head onto the trailer wheels and front vehicle wheels. This reduces the noseweight and affects the stability of the trailer – improving it if the noseweight is too high, reducing it if the noseweight is correct. Make allowance for this effect when loading your trailer.

● Some stabilisers cause a slight delay in the action of the overrun brakes because of the additional friction between the trailer and tow vehicle. Stabilisers that only control sideways movement do not have this problem.

Trailer suspension

All road-going trailers, except for some agricultural and forestry trailers, are required to have suspension units fitted between the wheels and the chassis. Both traditional leaf springs or the more recently introduced steel-cased rubber suspensions are fine. Car-type coil spring units are generally unable to cope with the loadings imposed by goods type trailers, and are only found on older 'nominal load' type trailers such as caravans.

Leaf springs and rubber suspensions have different characteristics. Leaf springs are more robust and therefore better suited to rough terrain. Rubber suspensions have better damping characteristics (fast deflection/slow return) producing a smoother drive on roads. Special suspensions have also been developed for uses such as the caravan market, where there is little difference between the unladen and the laden weight. These suspensions would not be suitable for uses such as a builder's trailer, where the variation in loading is significant. This requires a progressive suspension, one which starts off relatively soft but gets harder as the load increases.

The trailer suspension is an important determinant of the stability of the outfit. As there is no one best solution for all trailer uses, the right solution is achieved by getting a clear idea of what you want to use your trailer for, and seeking advice from trailer suspension manufacturers.

Incompatible suspensions

Trailer suspensions have characteristics similar to car suspensions, which minimises drawbar stress – both trailer and car suspensions respond to surface irregularities in similar ways. But the characteristics of some dual-purpose and light commercial vehicle suspensions are different from those of trailers. This can impose undue stresses on drawbars when these vehicles tow trailers over uneven surfaces. These stresses can be minimised by shock absorbing devices, which damp the vertical movement of the trailer nose and absorb some of the stresses.

Wheel hubs and bearings

The wheel bearings along with tyres and the braking system are the major source of trailer breakdowns. Trailer wheels often bear considerable loads and need to be well maintained to do what is required of them. Check hub bearings at least annually to ensure that they are in good order. Unless your bearings are of the sealed for life type, it is most important that you inspect and repack them with grease at the intervals recommended in your trailer handbook. Use a water repellent grease.

Boat trailers

Particular attention needs to be paid to boat trailer bearings. Warm wheels should never be immersed in water. If a hot bearing is immersed in cold water a vacuum is formed which sucks water into the bearing. This degrades the grease and rusts the bearing, and failure of the bearing is an inevitable consequence. Salt water accentuates the problems because of its corrosiveness.

If your boat trailer is of the type that requires the wheels to be immersed to launch the boat, consider taking professional advice on whether to replace the hubcap with a bearing saver. These maintain a constant pressure of grease within the hub cavity through a spring loaded piston, helping to prolong the life of the bearing. You are advised to check the bearings every time they are submerged.

Trailer lights and signs

See Chapter 1 for legal requirements.

Trailer lights must all work, and their lenses be kept clean. Tail lights, indicator lights and rear fog lights must not show any white light. Each time you hitch up check that all the trailer lights are working as required.

Mirrors

See Chapter 1 for legal requirements.

You are required to be able to see to the sides and rear of your trailer. If you cannot, fit additional wing mirrors or extensions to your existing mirrors. Some caravans have windows which are low enough to see right through using the rear view mirror.

Winches

Winches should be regularly lubricated and protected and covered when not in use. The handle should never be allowed to spin round as the cable is spooled out. Winches on trailers used in a work setting are covered by the Health and Safety at Work Act and should be automatically braked. It would also appear that EU Directives require manufacturers and retailers to supply only auto-braked winches for use in any setting, whether work or leisure.

Chapter 3

Getting ready to move

This chapter gives advice on getting your outfit ready to move and how to prevent and cope with instability. It assumes that your outfit is well-matched and well-maintained and that your load is within the tolerances of the outfit. A well-matched outfit has the following characteristics:

● the load is within the stated maximum load for the trailer

● the loaded trailer is within the stated maximum towing weight of the towing vehicle, and not more than 85% of its kerbside weight

● the recommended noseweight for the trailer is within or close to the maximum noseweight for the vehicle; the actual noseweight must never exceed the vehicle manufacturer's recommended noseweight

● the gross train weight of the outfit is less than the vehicle manufacturer's stated maximum gross train weight.

Loading the trailer

The weight that your towing vehicle can tow safely is limited. This limit is either stated in your vehicle handbook or is 85% of the vehicle's kerbside weight, whichever is less.

See Chapter 2, Weight

The outfit trailer payload – the weight that you can safely tow – depends on five things:

● your licence entitlements: See Chapter 1

● the towing capacity of your vehicle

● the unladen weight of your trailer

● the trailer manufacturer's stated maximum payload for the trailer

● the gross train weight of the towing vehicle as specified by the manufacturer.

The difference between your vehicle manufacturer's stated towing limit and the unladen weight of your trailer gives you the outfit trailer payload – the payload that you can safely tow with that particular vehicle and that particular trailer. But note that the outfit trailer payload must never exceed the trailer manufacturer's stated maximum payload.

Take for example a typical unbraked trailer:

gross weight	600kg
unladen weight	125kg
payload	**475kg**

And a typical middle-size family car:

kerbweight	1185kg
maximum unbraked trailer weight	590kg

vehicle maximum unbraked trailer weight		590kg
trailer unladen weight	–	125kg
	=	465kg
trailer maximum payload		**475kg**
outfit trailer payload	=	**465kg**

In this example the outfit trailer payload is 10kg less than the trailer manufacturer's maximum payload.

Taking a typical 4x4 offroad vehicle with the following
specifications:

	kerbweight	2000kg
	maximum unbraked trailer weight	750kg

And calculating the outfit trailer weight for towing the same
trailer as in the first example:

	vehicle maximum unbraked trailer weight		750kg
	trailer unladen weight		– 125kg
		=	625kg
trailer maximum payload			**475kg**
outfit trailer payload			**475kg**

Here the outfit trailer weight is limited by the payload capacity
of the trailer to 475kg; a stronger trailer would allow a heavier
load to be safely towed by this vehicle.

Gross train weight

The gross train weight (GTW) is another limitation that the
towing vehicle places on the trailer payload. Gross train weight
(also called gross combination weight, GCW) is the total weight
that the vehicle is designed to pull. It comprises the weight of
the vehicle, its occupants and its load, and the weight of the
trailer and its load. If you load the trailer up to its full capacity
you must make sure that the load you place in the vehicle does
not cause the combined weight of vehicle and trailer to exceed
the GTW. If it does you must either reduce the load in the
vehicle or in the trailer, until the combined weight is equal to or
less than the GTW. The GTW (or GCW) is marked on the VIN
plate, which is generally found in the vehicle's engine
compartment.

Use the table below to note down key details about your outfit, and to work out the maximum payload that you can safely tow.

Outfit weights and capacities

		Weight
	Name of vehicle:	
	Name of trailer:	
A	Towing vehicle's maximum towing weight or 85% of vehicle kerbside weight, whichever is less	
B	Trailer's unladen weight	
C	Maximum trailer payload as stated by the trailer manufacturer	
D	Outfit trailer payload (A minus B up to maximum of C)*	
E	Kerbside weight of vehicle	
F	Maximum authorised mass for vehicle	
G	Maximum payload for vehicle (F minus E)	
H	Actual vehicle weight (weight of vehicle + occupants + actual load)	
I	Actual trailer weight (weight of trailer + actual load)	
J	Actual gross train weight (H + I)	
K	Stated vehicle gross train weight (J must not exceed K)	
L	Vehicle's maximum noseweight	
M	Trailer's recommended noseweight	
N	Actual noseweight (N must never exceed L, N should be as close to M as is possible)	
O	Vehicle tyre pressures for towing — Front	
	Rear	
P	Trailer tyre pressures	

* The outfit trailer payload will be less than the maximum trailer payload if the maximum trailer payload exceeds the weight that the towing vehicle is designed to pull

63

Stowing the load

The loading of a trailer is critical to the stability of the outfit. An unbalanced trailer or a load that shifts in transit will make the outfit difficult and possibly dangerous to drive. The key considerations for the safe loading of a trailer are the weight of the load, the type of load, the positioning of the load, the noseweight and the securing of the load. Use the following guidelines for loading your trailer.

> **Guidelines for loading a trailer**
> Do not exceed the outfit trailer payload
> stow the load as low as possible
> distribute the load evenly over each axle
> place sufficient weight forward of the wheels to give the correct noseweight
> fully secure the load.

Calculating weights

It is important to have an accurate weight for the load you intend to tow. There are two ways to achieve this: totting up the weights of the separate elements or weighing the vehicle and trailer on a weighbridge.

Totting up

In this method simply add all the individual weights of load items, the trailer and the vehicle. Weights can be obtained by weighing the individual load items from standard tables of weights and from vehicle and trailer handbooks/plates:

- add up the weight of each item loaded onto the trailer to give you the **actual trailer payload**
- add the actual trailer payload to the unladen weight of the trailer to give **actual gross trailer weight**
- add the weight of each item loaded into the towing vehicle (including occupants) to give the **actual vehicle load**
- add the actual vehicle load to the kerbweight of the vehicle to give the **actual gross vehicle weight**
- add the gross trailer weight and the gross vehicle weight to give **actual gross train weight**.

Weighbridge

You can find out where your nearest public weighbridges are from your area Trading Standards Department (Weights and Measures). Look in the phone book for the Trading Standards telephone number.

Public weighbridges are generally used to weigh much heavier loads than those towed on light trailers and may give an inaccurate reading for your outfit. It is worthwhile discussing this with the weighbridge operator before choosing a particular weighbridge.

Load your vehicle and trailer with the standard load that you intend to carry, making a record of what is included. At the weighbridge, weigh your vehicle and trailer separately (make sure you have uncoupled vehicle and trailer or you will get a false reading). Get a written record of the individual weights from the operator.

Alternatively, some local caravan groups have their own portable weighing machines, which you may be able to use.

Type and position of load

Trailers that are designed to carry single-piece loads such as a boat or a car transporter will not necessarily be able to carry the same weight if it is made up of separate pieces. This is because a single load contributes its own rigidity to the trailer, whereas a split load does not.

When there is a split load with articles of different weights, put the heaviest pieces closest to the axle, leaving positions further away for lighter pieces. Also make sure that the load is evenly balanced on each side of the trailer, as well as front and back. If all the heavy items are placed on one side of the trailer it will be unbalanced and unstable. The ideal is to have a symmetrical distribution of weight about the axle, shifted sufficiently forward to achieve the correct noseweight. Keep the load as low as possible to keep the centre of gravity low and improve stability.

Single item loads should also be positioned as centrally as possible, so that the bulk of the weight is over the axle and the load is evenly distributed. With top-heavy loads, remove as much weight as possible from the top to lower the centre of gravity. Lashings used to prevent an object toppling over should be attached above the centre of gravity.

Packing a caravan

The large amount of space in a caravan makes it tempting to pack ever more items into it, but usually the payload of a caravan is fairly limited:

- the outfit trailer payload applies as much to caravans as it does to any other trailer – do not exceed it

- evenly distribute the weight of the load around the interior of the caravan, with as much weight as possible being over or slightly forward of the axle; try to keep the weight on each side of the caravan evenly balanced

- keep the weight as low down as possible

- the weight on each side of the caravan should be more or less equal; where possible counterbalance heavy fixed items such as a fridge or a cooker with heavy load items

- do not place heavy items at the rear of the caravan, even to achieve the correct noseweight; they increase the pendulum effect of any snaking, making it more difficult to regain control

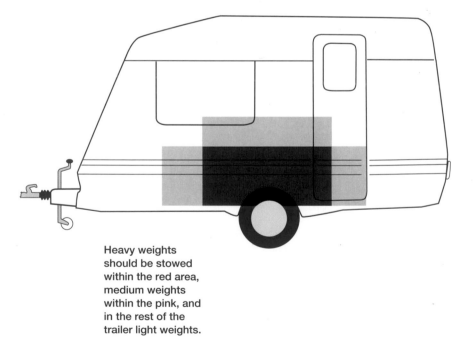

Heavy weights should be stowed within the red area, medium weights within the pink, and in the rest of the trailer light weights.

- empty any water containers/tanks/toilets – water is heavy, and fluids surging around inside a container reduce stability

- consider moving the spare wheel from the front locker to a central position over the wheels – if left at the front it might make the noseweight too heavy

- put heavy items such as awnings in the towing vehicle rather than the caravan – but do not exceed the weight limit for the vehicle

- only put lightweight items in the roof lockers

- make sure all movable items are well secured; shifting loads cause damage and destabilise the caravan

- measure the noseweight of the caravan after loading it – if it is too heavy, reduce or redistribute the load to achieve the correct weight.

Noseweight

Once the trailer is loaded, check the noseweight. It is important to have a noseweight that is heavy enough to ensure stability while not exceeding the manufacturers' maximum noseweight. Generally the noseweight should be between 50 and 100kg, your vehicle manual or the towbar plate will give the correct weight for your vehicle. Too light a noseweight will cause snaking; too heavy a noseweight risks damaging the towing vehicle or the trailer drawbar, and impairing steering.

General advice is that a caravan's noseweight should be about 7% of its actual laden weight, providing this figure does not exceed the noseweight recommendation for the towing vehicle or the trailer hitch.

See Chapter 2, Measuring the noseweight

The only way that you can be sure of the actual noseweight is to measure it.

Adjusting the noseweight

Measure and adjust the noseweight on a level surface, when everything is loaded for the journey:

- to increase the noseweight move the load closer to the drawbar

- to reduce the noseweight move the load away from the drawbar.

Securing the load

The Highway Code clearly states that it is the driver's responsibility to ensure that the load is secure and does not stick out dangerously. A load that shifts during a journey could destabilise the outfit, and one that falls off the trailer endangers other road users. Good quality ties are essential for securing a load – ratchet straps are generally preferable to ropes. Ratchet straps have a specified load capacity, are less likely to stretch, and can be pulled far tighter than ropes. They are also quicker to use. For heavy loads, such as machinery, chains may be necessary.

Advice on using ratchet straps

- check that the ratchet mechanism is undamaged before each use, never use a damaged mechanism

- check the strap for any wear or fraying, never use a damaged strap

- never attempt to repair or modify a ratchet strap yourself: return it to the manufacturer

- never tie knots in the strap

- never use a ratchet strap for lifting

- use sufficient straps for the load

- protect the straps from sharp edges.

Do not take risks with securing ties – if in doubt add extra ties or go up to ties with a higher load rating. Above all, never think to yourself that you will make up for insufficient ties by driving extra carefully or slowly.

Factors to consider when lashing

Stresses on ties occur when braking, cornering, bouncing and pulling away. One of the commonest ways of losing a load is for it to slip off the back of the trailer during pulling away. Braking forces are probably the strongest forces, so place your load against the headboard if you can do so and still maintain the correct noseweight. Think about these stresses when securing your load; you need to restrain forward movement, backward movement, up and down movement and sideways movement. Take extra care if there is little grip between the load and the trailer deck because the deck is greasy or the load is very smooth. Think also about the wind effects on the loads and lashings. Wind vibration of load and

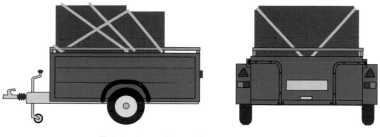

Think about the motion stresses when securing
your load; you need to restrain forward
movement, backward movement, up and down
movement and sideways movement.

lashings can fray or loosen the lashings. Protect the lashings from
sharp edges and use sheeting to prevent the wind getting in
between the load and causing it to vibrate.

Key tips on securing loads

- On flat bed trailers, keep the lashing to prevent forward/back
  movement as close to the deck as possible. The angle between
  lashing and deck should never be greater than 60°.
- Make sure that lashings hold onto the load at points above the
  load's centre of gravity.
- Timber can compress in transit. Check the lashings frequently
  and retighten them as necessary.
- Use side supports or banding to prevent stacks of boards and
  similar loads from concertinaing.
- Make sure that palletised loads are securely lashed to their
  pallet and that the pallet is sound. If possible, place the pallet
  against the headboard.
- Secure wheeled vehicles with wheel-ties and separate ties to
  the chassis to prevent it from bouncing. Make sure the ties do
  not crush brake/fuel pipes or wiring. Apply the vehicle
  handbrake and put in a low gear.
- Use tie sleeves at the point where ties are strapped round box
  sections or bars to protect the ties and equalise tension on
  both sides of the tie.
- Use restraint poles, which attach to the trailer sides to
  prevent loads shifting in box trailers. Cargo nets can also be
  used to quickly secure loads in a box trailer.

*Choose a safe
place to stop and
check your load
15 minutes after
the journey start
and 15 minutes
after joining a
motorway or fast
dual carriageway.*

Hitching up

Hitching large trailers is most easily accomplished if another person assists the driver and the towing vehicle is reversed to the trailer. Do not let children assist you. For small trailers, which can be moved by one person, it is easier to drag the trailer to the towing vehicle. Apart from this, the procedure is the same for any size of trailer. Try to adopt a standard routine for hitching your trailer; that way you are less likely to forget anything.

Hitching routine

- Ensure trailer and load are prepared for the road; with caravans check that doors, windows and skylights are locked and that the gas is turned off at the cylinder
- remove security devices and towball/electrical socket dustcaps
- check that the towball is adequately greased, unless you are using a towball-mounted friction stabiliser
- for a small trailer release the trailer handbrake and drag the trailer to the towball
- for a large trailer check that the trailer handbrake is applied and consider chocking the wheels if the trailer is on a slope
- lower the jockey wheel to raise the coupling head clear of the towball
- raise trailer corner steadies, if applicable
- position your assistant on the offside, to the side of the vehicle, and level with the coupling head
- align your vehicle with the trailer, using your mirrors to centre your vehicle on the trailer (if you can see the jockey wheel or handbrake handle through the rear window, use that to centre your vehicle)
- ask your assistant to talk/guide you into the hitch position, with the ball under the coupling head
- apply the vehicle handbrake, place in low gear and switch off engine
- lower the head onto the ball by raising the jockey wheel, holding the locking trigger if applicable
- check that the head is locked onto the ball through position of locking handle, audible click or visual indicator, as applicable
- lower jockey wheel and raise the towball a couple of winds to check that the head and ball are truly engaged

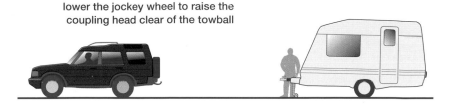

lower the jockey wheel to raise the coupling head clear of the towball

position your assistant on the offside, to the side of the vehicle, and level with the coupling head

lower the head onto the ball by raising the jockey wheel, holding the locking trigger if applicable

- fully raise and stow the jockey wheel
- connect the stabiliser, if applicable
- attach the breakaway cable or secondary coupling to a secure point on the towing vehicle
- connect the 12N and 12S plugs to the sockets; ensure that there is sufficient slack in the cables to allow turning, but not so much as to allow them to drag on the road
- if applicable, check on older trailers that the manual reverse lever is not engaged, if applicable
- release trailer handbrake
- adjust your wing and rearview mirrors to give you a good view along both sides and behind the trailer
- switch on vehicle ignition and ask assistant to help check that lights, brakelights and indicators are working
- adjust your wing and rearview mirrors to give you a good view along both sides and behind the trailer
- at the earliest safe opportunity after moving off check that the brakes are working.

Unhitching a trailer

As with hitching, establishing a standard routine for unhitching will help to ensure that all the necessary tasks are carried out.

● Find a relatively level surface to unhitch your trailer; trailer handbrakes are only required to be able to hold the trailer still on a maximum slope of 18%

● use the vehicle to position the trailer as accurately as possible in its final position, with the wheels mounted on whatever levelling blocks are necessary; manoeuvring large trailers by hand is heavy work

● if you have auto-reverse brakes, make the final movement in a forwards direction to ensure that the trailer brakes are re-engaged

● pull the trailer handbrake fully on

● chock the trailer wheels if parked on a slope

● disconnect the electrical cables

● remove the stabiliser, if appropriate

Avoiding back injury

Lifting and moving a trailer, which does not have a jockey wheel, may cause back injury. It is best for one person to lift the nose of the trailer and another to move it.

● unlock the coupling, and using the jockey wheel raise the coupling head off the towball

● disconnect the breakaway/secondary coupling cable, but do not do this while the trailer is coupled

● drive the towing vehicle clear, and park safely

● use the jockey wheel to level front and back of the trailer

● lower the corner steadies, if applicable

● fit anti-theft devices to the trailer, if applicable

● if the trailer is to be parked for a long time, chock the wheels and release the trailer handbrake to prevent the brakeshoes sticking to the drums.

A trailer may not be left on a highway at night without lighting.

See Chapter 1,
Traffic law.

Tyres

See Chapter 2,
Tyres.

After loading your trailer and hitching it to the loaded vehicle, check the vehicle and trailer tyre pressures. It is essential that they are correct. While checking the pressures take the opportunity to inspect the tyres for signs of cracking or other damage, and to inspect the trailer wheel nuts for tightness.

Next, compare the bulge on the tyres to check that the load is evenly distributed between the axles. Excessive bulging of any one tyre or set of tyres indicates that the load is not evenly distributed between wheels/axles, and may exceed their individual capacities. If there is uneven bulging of the tyres, consider the need to redistribute or reduce the load.

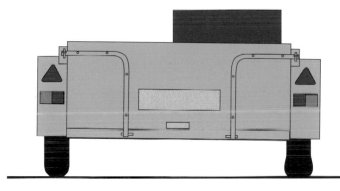

Excessive bulging of any one tyre or set of tyres indicates that the load is not evenly distributed.

Posture

After hitching the trailer to the vehicle check the posture of vehicle and trailer. This needs to be done on level ground, with the vehicle and trailer carrying their full load, including passengers, for the journey.

The trailer should be level or slightly nose down. If the vehicle sags excessively at the rear, correct it by removing some weight from the rear of the vehicle (do not reduce noseweight unless it is excessive). Excessive rear-end sag seriously destabilises the vehicle. The outfit should not be driven until the fundamental suspension problems are resolved.

See Chapter 2,
Suspension

If the trailer is nose up because of insufficient noseweight it will remove grip from the rear tyres of the vehicle, and destabilise the outfit. If it is nose up because of too high a hitching point on the vehicle, it will overburden the vehicle's rear suspension and reduce tyre grip at the front wheels, again reducing outfit stability. In both cases it will put an excessive load on the rear axle of a double axled trailer.

The fifteen minute check

Fifteen minutes after starting your journey, find a safe place to stop where you will not be a danger to yourself or other road users and carry out the following checks.

● Check the load is fully secure and all the ties are fully taut. Re-tighten as necessary.

● Check that the trailer tyres are still properly inflated and the tyre walls are reasonably cool.

● Check that the wheel centres are reasonably cool. If they are not it could mean that the brakes are binding or that the wheel bearings need greasing or adjusting. Both causes require immediate attention. Bearings in need of maintenance could fail at any moment with the loss of a wheel; binding brakes destabilise the outfit.

● You are also recommended to repeat the test, 15 minutes after moving onto a motorway or other dual carriageway where you travel at sustained high speeds. The sustained high speeds put loads, lashings and wheel bearings under increased stress. Leave the carriageway and find a safe place, such as a service station or lay-by, to conduct the check. Unless there is an emergency do not stop on the hard shoulder of a motorway.

Preventing and coping with instability

This section looks at the causes of snaking, how to prevent it, and what to do should it occur. All outfits experience some tail swing while towing – small, sideways movements of the trailer's tail – but in a well-balanced outfit this movement is self damping and rapidly discontinues. The driver quickly learns to recognise it as part of the normal operation of the trailer. Snaking occurs when the tail swing intensifies instead of lessening – an abnormal and highly dangerous situation. Very quickly, the pendulum effect of the trailer grows and starts to pull the towing vehicle from side to side. Unchecked, the whole outfit becomes destabilised and uncontrollable.

What are the causes of snaking?

Anything which destabilises the outfit contributes to snaking:

- a fundamental cause is an ill-matched outfit. If the trailer is too heavy for the towing vehicle the outfit will be unstable and prone to snaking. It is recommended that the actual laden weight of the trailer should not exceed 85% of the kerbweight of the towing vehicle, or the manufacturer's recommended maximum towing weight, whichever is the less. *See Chapter 2*

- incorrect height of tow hitch. *See Chapter 2*

- incorrectly inflated or unbalanced tyres. *See Chapter 2*

- badly maintained or adjusted trailer brakes. *See Chapter 2*

- overloaded trailer or unbalanced loading of the trailer. *See Chapter 3*

- incorrect noseweight. *See Chapter 3*

- driving too fast. The faster you drive the more you accentuate any instabilities in your outfit.

- driving fast downhill: trailers are less stable when going downhill. *See Chapter 9*

- strong gusts of wind blowing the trailer sideways
- road surface irregularities deflecting the wheels of the trailer
- fast high sided vehicles causing buffeting, suction and windbreak effects.

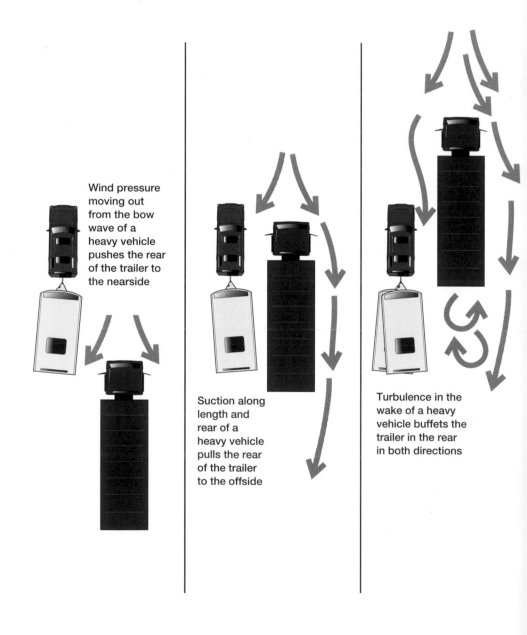

Wind pressure moving out from the bow wave of a heavy vehicle pushes the rear of the trailer to the nearside

Suction along length and rear of a heavy vehicle pulls the rear of the trailer to the offside

Turbulence in the wake of a heavy vehicle buffets the trailer in the rear in both directions

How to prevent snaking

Preventing snaking is much better than trying to recover control once it occurs.

- Only use a well-maintained, correctly laden, well-matched outfit, with correct tyre pressures and the correct noseweight. *See Chapters 2 and 3.*

- Fit a stabiliser, but only if the outfit is fundamentally sound

- Drive at a speed appropriate for the outfit and the conditions – reduce speed going down hills and in windy conditions. *See Chapters 5 and 9*

- Keep a careful lookout for large sided vehicles (especially coaches) approaching to overtake you. As they draw level with the rear of your trailer, move as far over to the nearside of your lane as is safe and possible. If you see your tail end start to sway, ease off the acceleration.

- If you have experienced some sway, take the first safe opportunity to stop. Examine and rearrange your load and check your tyre pressures and noseweight.

How to recover from snaking

If despite all the above precautions you do get into a snake, follow these guidelines:

- release the accelerator to allow engine compression to slow down the outfit

- hold the steering wheel firmly, steering straight ahead. Let the wheel twitch in your hands

- do not brake – EXCEPT when going down hill, and then brake gently to reduce speed smoothly

- do not use sharp movements of the steering in an attempt to counteract the swings – it will make matters worse

- do not attempt to accelerate out of the snake; it does not work.

After recovering from the snake reconsider whether your outfit is as well-matched or well-maintained as you believed.

Chapter 4

Towing different types of trailer

This chapter gives advice for specific trailer types. This advice is in addition to the general advice contained in the rest of the book and should be read with it. The types covered are:

- boat trailers
- caravans
- horse trailers
- general purpose trailers.

Boat trailers

Make sure that your boat trailer is strong enough and big enough to carry your boat. Do not forget to include the weight of the outboard motor and any other accessories for the boat when you are checking that the actual load is within the maximum trailer load and that the total trailer load is within the stated maximum towing weight of the towing vehicle.

As with any other trailer, boat trailers should have the correct noseweight to reduce the likelihood of snaking.

Boat trailers are limited to a maximum width of 2.3m like any other trailer. If the boat overhangs the rear of the trailer it is required to have a lighting board of adequate width, and to comply with other marking regulations. Boat trailers have certain exemptions from marker light requirements.

See Chapter 1, Size of trailers; Number plate; Projecting loads; Lights, indicators and triangles.

Any propellers that stick out at the back of the boat need to be covered, and extra care needs to be taken with a long mast to avoid hitting low bridges, lamp-posts, trees or the roof of the towing vehicle on sharp inclines.

Boat trailer bearings

Boat trailers suffer from exposure to water, salt and sand. If you put hot wheels into cool water a vacuum is created inside the bearings. The vacuum sucks water past the seals and causes serious damage to the bearings. You then run the risk of losing a wheel while in transit.

Don't put a hot wheel into cold water; always let the bearings cool down first.

Fitting bearing savers to the hubs of boat trailers helps to reduce the problem. These are loaded with grease which is pressurised by a spring. The spring forces grease into the bearings should any vacuum develop. There is a view that bearing savers should not be fitted to braked wheels for fear of contaminating the friction linings with grease if the bearing seals should fail. Take professional advice. Better still, avoid placing the trailer wheels in water by using a trailer with a removable wheeled boat carrier. These lightweight wheeled frames sit on the trailer and are used to transport the boat between trailer and water.

American boat trailers

Many American boats imported into the UK come with a free trailer. Many of these trailers are too wide to be towed by a vehicle under 3.5 tonne GVW, and fail to meet UK regulations. They generally have:

- two inch coupling heads or unsafe universal type coupling heads
- no breakaway cable
- hydraulic or electric brakes
- no parking brakes
- aluminium wheels
- American lights, which are all red.

Such trailers cannot legally be used on UK roads.

Winches

Winches are commonly used to haul boats onto trailers. Winches can be very dangerous if their handles flail around when paying out the load, or if they suddenly fail under the load and release the cable. Winches used in a work situation must comply with health and safety legislation. They must be automatically braked in addition to any ratchet mechanism they might have. EU Directives would appear to require that manufacturers and retailers supply only auto-braked winches for use in any setting, either work or leisure. Generally, trailer winches should not be used for straight vertical lifts. They are designed to haul loads along a surface, and their capacities are calculated accordingly.

Guidelines for using winches

- Make sure the winch can pull in a straight line without the cable/strap fouling on the trailer
- frayed, corroded, crushed or otherwise damaged winch cables must be replaced immediately
- make sure any replacement winch cables/straps have the same specification as the original item – check breaking strength and width specifically
- wind the cable onto the drum in even layers; the bulkier the windings, the lower the mechanical advantage
- regularly clean and regrease the winch mechanism
- keep wire winch cables lightly oiled
- the only user-replaceable parts of most winches are the cables and the handles; if other parts are worn out, replace the complete winch.

Caravans

About one fifth of trailers on the road are caravans. They are often irregularly used and parked up for most of the winter. This pattern of use gives rise to specific maintenance problems, and can mean that drivers take some time to become experienced towers. Caravans are generally much bulkier than other types of trailer, making them more difficult to manoeuvre and reducing visibility to the rear. However, provided they follow the advice of matching big vehicle with small trailer, most drivers are pleasantly surprised to find how easily a caravan moves.

See Chapter 3, Packing a caravan and Hitching up.

Use only well-balanced and well-maintained outfits

● Only use a well-balanced outfit – one where the maximum laden weight of the caravan is less than the vehicle's maximum towing weight or less than 85% of the kerbside weight of the towing vehicle, whichever is less.

● After the winter storage, check and service the coupling mechanism, brakes, hub bearings, tyres, suspension and electrical system. Inside the caravan check and service the electrical, gas and water systems and equipment. Always ensure that the wheel bearings are adequately greased and the brakes work properly.

● Fit mirror extensions to give you a good view along each side of the caravan and behind.

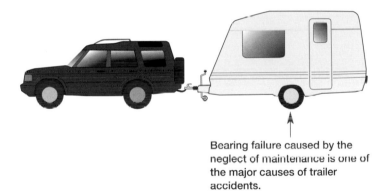

Bearing failure caused by the neglect of maintenance is one of the major causes of trailer accidents.

Before moving

See Chapter 3, Packing a caravan.

● Avoid the temptation to overload your caravan or towing vehicle. Basic items for a caravan trip weigh at least 50kg plus 25kg per person.

● Ensure you have the correct noseweight, which for optimum stability in a caravan is generally recommended to be 7% of actual laden weight, providing this does not exceed the towing vehicle's limit.

● Do not overload the boot or pile luggage high on the roof rack of a towing car: it will destabilise the car and the outfit.

● Once the caravan is hitched, check that the outfit is level, or slightly dipping to the hitch. Make sure the headlights are level.

- Check the tyre pressures of the whole outfit. Uneven or low pressures causes snaking.

- Hitch the caravan in a standard way, so as not to forget anything.

  . *See Chapter 3, Hitching up.*

- Make sure you know the regulations governing speed, lane use and lighting requirements.

- Turn off the gas supply, and lock doors and windows.

- Never allow anyone to travel in the caravan.

On the road

Remember your outfit is longer, heavier and slower than when driving solo. You need to:

- Increase your observation and plan your actions further ahead.

- Allow more time and space for manoeuvres.

- Allow more space on the inside of corners for trailer cutting – trailers do not follow the vehicle's front wheels round corners, they take the shortest route. Also be aware of 'end swing' on large caravans. As you change direction going round a corner the caravan pivots about its wheels and its end swings out – make sure there is enough clearance behind and to the outside of the caravan's sweep to avoid hitting any other road user or object.

- Because of the greater weight, braking will take longer. Allow more distance for braking – you should always drive at a speed which allows you to stop in the distance you can see to be clear.

- Increase the following distance between you and the vehicle in front to allow for the greater braking distances.

- Use your mirrors to check for cyclists or other road users on the inside of your outfit when turning a corner. Regularly check mirrors to assess the position of following traffic and to identify the approach of large, high-sided vehicles which may cause turbulence. If a queue of following traffic builds up behind you, pull in and let them past.

- Reduce speed in strong cross winds, when going down hill and in poor visibility.

- Take regular rest breaks – at least every two hours. Take the opportunity to check couplings, tyres and wheel hubs for overheating.

Gas precautions

Liquefied Petroleum Gas (LPG) is of its nature a hazardous substance, and extra precautions need to be taken when transporting it.

- Turn off the gas at the bottle before any journey.

- You are strongly recommended not to run your fridge off bottled gas during transit. Naked flames are forbidden at petrol stations, service areas and in most tunnels.

- Gas bottles must be kept upright during transport and at other times. All cylinders should be properly secured in cradles during transport and at other times.

- Ship and tunnel operators have restrictions on the transport of LPG. Contact the operator to find out how much LPG you are permitted to carry and what precautions you are required to take.

Snaking

See Chapter 3 Preventing and coping with instability

Snaking is a particular problem for caravans because they are 'air-boxes' and easily destabilised by the suction of passing trucks. Comprehensive advice on this problem is given in Chapter 3.

Horse trailers

Horses can be heavy animals; when their weight is added to that of the trailer, the trailer's actual laden weight is likely to exceed 85% of the kerbweight of most cars. The closer the actual laden weight of the trailer approaches the kerbside weight of the towing vehicle, the more unstable the outfit will become. In addition to this, horses move around, further destabilising the trailer. It is therefore critically important that maximum weights are calculated before an outfit is put together.

The maximum weight of the heaviest horse(s) you are going to carry should be added to the unladen weight of the trailer. This must not exceed either the trailer's maximum gross weight or the maximum towing weight of the towing vehicle. If you exceed these limits you put at risk your own life, and the lives of other road users and your animal(s).

Horse trailers should be thoroughly washed down and disinfected after each use, as urine is extremely corrosive. It is also better to store the trailer on hard standing rather than on a field, because the humidity of the turf promotes corrosion.

Calculating weights

You can get a reasonably accurate estimate of the weight of your horse by using a weigh tape available from equestrian suppliers. In the absence of a weigh tape you can use the following calculation:

Weight in kilograms = (girth in cm)^2 x (length in cm) ÷ 8717

It is often difficult to measure the noseweight of a trailer loaded with horses because of their movements. As the horses move forwards and back a whole range of noseweight readings could be taken. Which then is the correct reading? It is simplest to use the trailer manufacturer's estimate of noseweight, and perhaps take some noseweight measurements to confirm that this is a reasonable estimate.

Horse trailer regulations

Horse trailers must have:

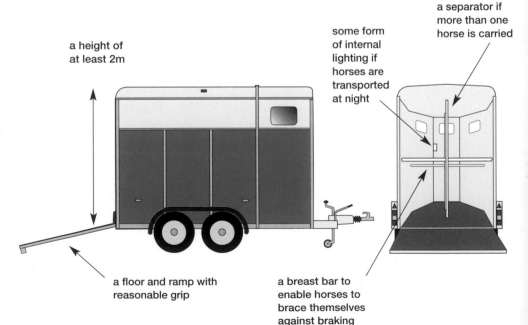

a separator if more than one horse is carried

some form of internal lighting if horses are transported at night

a height of at least 2m

a floor and ramp with reasonable grip

a breast bar to enable horses to brace themselves against braking

Preparing your horse for the journey

- Use a leather headcollar which will break should the horse become entangled during the journey.

- Protective clothing, including a tailguard or bandage, is recommended to prevent injury during transit.

- Use a rug which fits well and is appropriate for the temperature.

On the move

Besides road safety considerations, you have your animal's welfare to consider. Imagine being confined in a container with restricted views, only slightly larger than you; then being swung and jostled and bumped. If you want your horse to enter the trailer again make the ride as smooth as possible.

- Drive very steadily and smoothly. This depends on good observation, anticipation and planning, and smooth acceleration, gear changing, braking and cornering. Imagine you have to drive smoothly enough to keep a tumbler of water placed on your dashboard from spilling.

- Take roundabouts very slowly; horses find the sudden changes in direction difficult to cope with.

- As the animals move, the noseweight and therefore the stability of the trailer will alter. Make allowances for this in your driving, adopting safety margins which can accommodate a sudden loss of stability.

- Never unload horses on the road.

- Be very careful about changing a tyre on the trailer or towing vehicle while horses are loaded. The movements of the horse can knock the vehicle or trailer off the jack.

- A mobile phone allows you to call for help in an emergency without leaving your animals.

- Drive very slowly off road. The suspension on trailers does not match that on modern vehicles; the ride will be much rougher for your horse than you. Drive slowly and avoid ruts and potholes. Driving quickly over rough ground might not only hurt your horse; it could damage the towbar, suspension, coupling head and wheel alignment of your trailer and vehicle.

Carriage of other live animals

There is separate legislation regulating the Carriage of Animals and Cattle, Calves, Pigs and Poultry. Generally this legislation requires that: the trailer is clean and disinfected; the animals are fit; they are loaded using an appropriate ramp; appropriately sized pens are constructed inside the trailer, horses are tethered and separated by dividers (except for mare and foal); and that the animals are fed and watered at least every eight hours.

General purpose trailers

Because of the variety of objects carried in general purpose trailers it is difficult to give specific advice. General advice is:

● Although it is permissible to tow unbraked trailers up to 750kg MAM, many towing organisations recommend that only braked trailers are used.

● Keep your trailer well maintained and have it serviced annually.

● Do not exceed the maximum weight limits for your trailer or towing vehicle.

● Ensure your trailer has the correct noseweight.

● Secure the load in your trailer carefully. Take particular care over securing timber loads and stacks of sheet materials.

See Chapter 3, Securing the load.

● Check and, if necessary, resecure your load 15 minutes after the journey's start and regularly thereafter.

● A tarpaulin with a 30cm overlap at each side will provide a means of securing light loose materials in a trailer and of protecting the inside of the trailer from the weather both in transit and in storage.

Chapter 5

Observation, anticipation, and planning skills

The basis of good towing is sound driving technique, and the skills of observation, anticipation and planning are the basis of sound driving. In this chapter we look at how these skills can improve your towing technique. The second part of the chapter looks at the effect of the weather on observation.

Why you need good observation skills

The additional length, width and weight of an outfit reduce its responsiveness to steering, accelerating and braking. To compensate for this you need to plan your driving further ahead: the key to planning is observation.

Observation depends on using your senses and experience to gain as much information about driving conditions as possible. Good observation gives you extra time to think and react, and so gives you more control over your outfit.

You may occasionally have caught yourself driving absent-mindedly, musing on anything but your driving, and only noticing what is happening immediately in front of you. In this state you are vulnerable – unprepared to deal with a sudden emergency, and potentially the victim of other road users' actions. You may also be a source of danger yourself because you are unaware of what other road users are doing. Safe towing requires you to actively attend to your driving all the time.

Planning

Safe towing depends on using your observations to plan your driving. Planning is a continuous process; as new hazards arise you need to take on board the new information and adjust your plans accordingly. It is helpful to look at planning in three stages:

- anticipate
- prioritise
- decide.

The aim of the plan is to put you in the right position, at the right speed, in the right gear, at the right time to negotiate hazards safely and efficiently.

The diagram illustrates the link between observation, planning and actions:

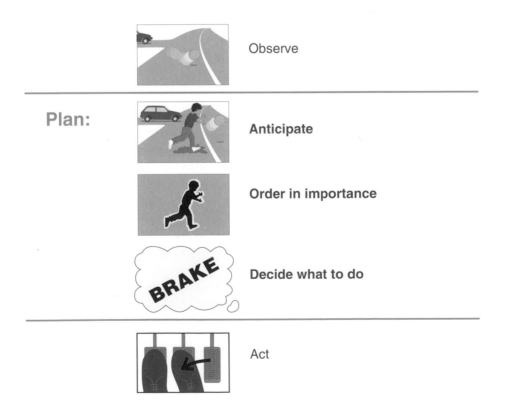

Observe

Plan: Anticipate

Order in importance

Decide what to do

Act

Now let's look more closely at the three activities in planning.

Anticipate

Anticipating hazards gives you more time to deal with them safely. Skill in anticipating depends on training, experience and how much effort you are willing to put into developing your ability to anticipate. One technique for improving anticipation is talking yourself through your driving. As you drive, talk through the hazards you observe, how you anticipate they will develop and what you propose to do about them.

Anticipating the actions of other road users is critical for safety. Never assume that other road users have either seen you or are going to react according to the *Highway Code*. Watch other drivers' general progress and road behaviour to get some idea of what sort of driver they are. But always be aware that even the most conscientious drivers can make mistakes.

Carefully watching other drivers' eye, hand and head movements will give you some idea of their intentions. However, always allow a safety margin of time and space to allow for mistakes. If you have a serious accident, being in the right is small consolation.

Prioritise

Decide which hazards are significant, and which are the most important. Grade the risks, and deal with them in order of importance. The priority of a hazard may change rapidly, so be ready to change your plans accordingly.

How dangerous a hazard is depends on:

- what it is
- how close it is to you
- its speed and its direction
- your speed and direction
- the road layout and road surface conditions
- your room for manoeuvre.

See Chapter 6, The system of driving control.

Deal with the most dangerous hazards first. This may seem obvious, but many drivers have swerved to avoid a cat only to collide with an oncoming vehicle.

Decide

When you have prioritised the hazards you are in a position to decide on your course of action. The aim of your plan is to ensure the safety of yourself and other road users at all times. A well-judged course of action takes account of:

● what can be seen

● what cannot be seen

● what might reasonably be expected to happen

● which hazards represent the greatest threat

● what to do if things turn out differently from expected (contingency plans).

If you plan your towing you should be able to take driving decisions methodically and without hesitation. While you are towing you should be continuously anticipating, ranking hazards in importance and deciding what to do. At first you might find it difficult to consciously work through the three stages, but with practice it will become second nature and prove a quick and reliable guide to action.

Remember:

● anticipate

● prioritise

● decide.

Generally, things do not just happen, they take a while to develop – good planning depends on early observation and early anticipation of risk.

Grading a hazard in terms of risk

The chart below shows five different risk situations.

Risk scale	Your action
1 A car pulls out at a junction as you draw level, turning left and joining your path.	Here the risk is a positive danger requiring drastic action to avoid a collision. Brake hard and move out if possible. No time to sound the horn – in fact the use of the horn may be counter-productive. The driver of the car may brake.
2 A car is stationary at the junction and angled to turn left. The driver has not looked in your direction. The brake lights go off and the car begins to move.	This situation contains serious risk. Alter your position if you have not already done so and lose speed sharply. Make a long horn note.
3 A car is on its final approach to the junction, slowing as if to stop, but you do not have eye contact with the driver.	The driver of the car is unaware of your presence. The risk is a real one. The driver may pull out. Alter your course to maximise the distance between you and the other car, and alter your speed. Consider a short horn note.
4 A car comes into view approaching the junction from the left.	The presence of the car represents a slight risk. Consider altering your position and speed.
5 Road junction is free of traffic.	Every road junction poses a risk. This junction is clear and vision is good. No action is required other than to keep making vision scans until the potential risk passes.

Improving your observation skills

Scanning

Use your eyes to build up a picture of what is happening all around you, as far as you can see, in every direction. The best way to build this picture is to use your eyes in a scanning motion which sweeps the whole environment: the distance, the mid-ground, the foreground, the sides and rear. Drivers who scan the environment looking for different kinds of hazard have a lower risk of accidents than drivers who concentrate their view on one area. Develop the habit of scanning repeatedly and regularly.

Scanning is a continuous process. When a new view opens out in front of you, scan the scene. By scanning the whole of the environment you will know where the areas of risk are. Check and recheck these risk areas in your visual sweeps. Avoid staring at particular risk areas because this stops you placing them in the broader context. Use your mirrors frequently, and consider checking over your shoulder when it is not safe to rely on your mirrors alone – for example, when moving off from the kerb, changing lanes, or moving round a roundabout.

Routine scanning enables you to spot all areas of risk, which you should then check and re-check.

Rear observation

Constantly use your mirrors to check what is going on behind you. If you can use your rearview mirror to look through the windows of your trailer, or through gaps in the load, do so to check what is directly behind. It is important to have a clear view behind and along each side of your trailer. If your trailer is long and obscures your rearview mirror, fit extension mirrors to both sides of your vehicle to ensure an adequate view. Besides using the mirrors to check the road situation, regularly use it to cast an eye over the trailer and its load to make sure everything is sound. Also use your mirror to check your trailer for tail-end sway in situations where snaking might develop.

You should be aware of any blindspots not covered by your mirrors. If you are checking your mirrors regularly enough (every few seconds), you should know if vehicles are occupying or moving into these areas. You can reduce the area of blind spot by moving your head and/or looking over your shoulder.

Use judgement in deciding when to look behind. Obviously when you are looking behind you are not looking ahead. This could be hazardous if, for example, you are close to the vehicle in front or if you have moved out to overtake. Equally there are situations when it is dangerous not to look behind, such as a right turn into a minor road.

In slow moving traffic, regularly check the nearside mirrors for the possibility of cyclists or pedestrians moving up on your nearside, especially if you intend to turn left.

Use peripheral vision

Peripheral vision is the area of eyesight surrounding the central area of sharply defined vision. Learn to react to your peripheral vision as well as your central vision. The eye's receptors in this area are different from the central receptors, and are particularly good at sensing movement. This helps to alert us to areas that need to be examined more closely. Peripheral vision gives us our sense of speed and lateral position, registers the movement of other road users and acts as a cue for central vision. It is the first area of sight to diminish as we grow tired.

How speed affects observation

At 60mph the shortest distance in which you can react and stop in a car is 73 metres (240 feet). This is the equivalent of 18 car lengths. The stopping distance for an outfit is greater, depending on the load and the efficiency of the trailer's brakes.

To anticipate events at speed you need to scan everything between your vehicle and the horizon.

- At speed, vibration can distort vision.

- The faster you go the further you need to look ahead. As your speed increases, consciously look beyond the point where your eyes naturally come to rest to allow yourself sufficient time to react.

- Fatigue limits your ability to see. When you are tired slow down and take a rest.

- Speed increases the distance you travel before you can react to what you have seen. You need to build this into your safe stopping distance. **When you double your speed you quadruple your braking distance**.

- Your ability to take in foreground detail decreases with speed and increases as you slow down. In areas of high traffic density such as town centres, you must slow down to be able to take in all the information necessary to drive safely.

Adjust your speed according to how well you can see, the complexity of the situation and the distance it will take you to stop. You must always be able to stop within the distance you can see to be clear.

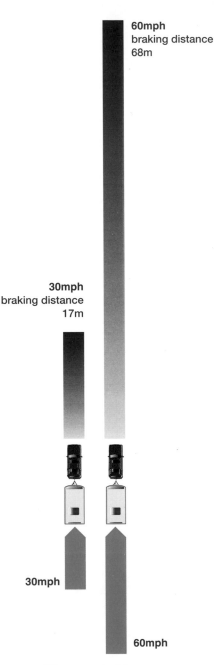

60mph braking distance 68m

30mph braking distance 17m

30mph

60mph

When you double your speed you quadruple your braking distance

Zones of visibility

The road around you is made up of different zones of visibility. In some areas your view will be good and in others you will only be able to see what is immediately in front of you. Where your view is restricted, use alternative sources of information, making the most of any glimpses of wider views that you can get. Typical areas with restricted views are junctions in towns and winding lanes in the country.

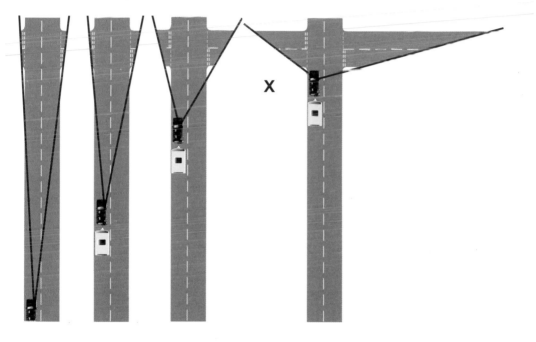

The illustration shows an outfit approaching a crossroads with a restricted view. For much of the approach the view improves very little, requiring the driver to approach the hazard with great care. From point X the view into the crossroads improves rapidly, allowing the driver to observe the position and behaviour of other road users. The driver now has the necessary information to decide whether to continue, stop, slow down or accelerate.

95

When you approach a hazard where your view is restricted, position your outfit to get the best view that is consistent with safety. Use every opportunity to get more information about the road ahead. Take every opportunity, however brief, to improve your observation of converging roads. Open spaces and breaks in hedges, fences or walls present opportunities. It is often possible to assess the severity of a bend or gradient by the position of trees, hedges or lamp-posts. The illustration shows how views open and close on the approach to a junction.

open spaces and breaks in hedges, fences and walls on the approach to a blind junction

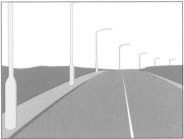

the curvature of a row of lamp-posts or trees

reflections in shop windows

the angle of approaching headlights

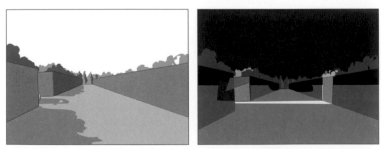

moving shadow or light cast by low sunlight or headlights.

Next time you drive along a familiar route, make a mental note of the opportunities to use additional sources of information.

Keep your distance – improve your view

Other vehicles affect how much you can see. The closer you are to the vehicle in front the less you will be able to see beyond it, especially if it is large or long. Slight adjustments in your road position, dropping back or moving sideways, can greatly improve your view. In slow-moving traffic drop back slightly and take views along both sides so that you can see what is happening two or three vehicles in front.

On motorways it is vital to have a good view of the road ahead because of the speeds involved. Your view will depend on the curvature and gradient of the carriageway, the lane that you are in, the size and position of other vehicles and your viewing height. Allowing for these, always keep back far enough from the vehicle in front to maintain a safe following distance. Avoid sitting in the blind spot of other vehicles, either overtake briskly or drop back. Check over your right shoulder to make sure that no one is sitting in your own blind spot before you move into the second lane. Some lorry drivers will flash their headlights to indicate that it is safe for you to move back into lane one when you have passed them. Always check carefully in your nearside mirror that it is in fact safe to move back.

When you are following a large lorry you will need to keep well back and take views to both sides of the vehicle.

Do you know exactly where the offside and nearside blind spots are on your outfit when fitted with towing mirrors? When you have a safe opportunity sit in your normal driving position and look through the mirrors. Identify the areas to the nearside, the offside and behind that you cannot see into. Move your head and look over your over your right shoulder to reduce the blind spots to a minimum.

Weather conditions

The weather affects how far you can see, and how your vehicle performs, so it is central to your observation and driving plan. When weather conditions reduce visibility, reduce your speed. Regularly check your actual speed on the speedometer. You must always be able to stop within the distance you can see to be clear.

Examples of weather conditions that reduce visibility are:

● fog and mist

● heavy rain

● snow and sleet

● bright sunshine.

Use of lights in bad weather

Choose your lights according to the circumstances.

● Switch on your dipped headlights when visibility is poor in daylight or fading light. This is particularly important in fog or heavy rain in daylight, when sidelights are virtually invisible.

● Generally you should use your dipped headlights and trailer lights whenever your wipers are in constant use.

● When there is fog or falling snow at night, foglights often give a better view than dipped headlights. Use them as an alternative to or together with dipped headlights.

● Switch off your rear foglights when you leave the fog in order not to dazzle following drivers.

● Do not use your main headlight beam when you are behind another vehicle in fog – it may dazzle the driver, and will cast a shadow of the vehicle on the fog ahead, disrupting the driver's view.

● Remember that the brilliance of rear foglights masks brakelights – allow more distance between you and the vehicle in front and aim to brake gently yourself.

Using your instruments in bad weather

Make full use of your washers and wipers to keep your windscreen as clear as possible. When there is a possibility of freezing fog consider whether it is sensible to venture out with a trailer at all. If you do, put freeze-resistant screen wash in the screen wash reservoir. In fog, rain, or snow regularly check your speedometer for your actual speed. You cannot rely on your eyes to judge speed accurately in these conditions. Low visibility distorts your perception of speed.

Observing when visibility is low

When visibility is low, keep to a slow steady pace and use the edge of the carriageway, hazard lines and cat's eyes as a guide, especially when approaching a road junction or corner. Staring into featureless mist tires the eyes very quickly. Focus instead on what you can see: the vehicle in front, the edge of the road or the road ahead. Avoid fixing your focus on the tail lights of the vehicle in front because they will tend to draw you towards it. You could collide if it stopped suddenly. Be ready to use your horn to inform other road users of your presence.

Always be prepared for a sudden stop in the traffic ahead. Do not follow closely, and only overtake other traffic when you can see that it is absolutely safe to do so. This is seldom possible in fog on a two-way road, especially when you are towing a trailer. At junctions when visibility is low, wind down your window and listen for other vehicles, and consider using your horn.

Weather and the road surface

Besides affecting visibility, the weather will also affect the road surface. Snow, rain or ice will greatly reduce the grip of the tyres, making skids and aquaplaning more likely. It takes up to ten times the normal distance to stop in icy or snowy conditions. Given the virtual impossibility of recovering an outfit from a skid, you are strongly recommended not to tow in ice or snow. Also remember that the inertia braking system on the trailer is less likely to be activated in slippery conditions, especially when the trailer is empty or partially laden.

Be aware that special hazards exist in summer. Dust on the road reduces tyre grip. Rain may produce a slippery road surface especially after a long dry spell.

The weather and motorways

Poor weather conditions can reduce visibility and road holding. At high speed the effects of these hazards are increased. When visibility is restricted you must reduce speed and consider using

headlights and foglights. You must use them if visibility drops
below 100 metres. A useful guide for assessing visibility is the
gap between motorway marker posts, which is approximately
100 metres. Bear in mind that foglights can mask the brake
lights and dazzle the driver behind and you must switch them
off when visibility improves.

Fog

Fog is particularly dangerous on motorways. It reduces drivers'
perception of speed and their perception of risk because they
cannot see; at the same time it encourages them to drive closer
together in order to keep sight of the vehicle lights ahead. Be
alert to the risks from the reckless behaviour of other drivers.

In freezing fog, mist and spray rapidly freezes on to the
windscreen at higher speeds and further reduces visibility. To
stop in the distance you can see to be clear in variable fog you
must adjust your speed to the actual density of the fog banks
you are driving through, not to some imagined 'safe' speed for
foggy conditions. Driving in fog is extremely tiring, so watch for
signs of fatigue and take more rest if necessary.
See also the fog code in the *Highway Code*.

Rain

At speed the hazards from rain and water lying on the surface of
the road increase. Heavy spray caused by tyres cutting through
water can reduce visibility to a few feet, and you should allow
for this, especially while overtaking. Water lying on the road
surface can build up to form a wedge of water between the tyres
and the road, causing aquaplaning: this results in instantaneous
and complete loss of control.

Hot spells

After a long, hot, dry spell a deposit of tyre and other dust
builds up on the road surface. These deposits create a slippery
surface especially during and after rain. Take precautions to
retain tyre grip in these conditions – reduce your speed and use
your controls very smoothly.

Snow and sleet

Snow and sleet reduce visibility and reduce tyre traction,
presenting particular difficulties for outfits. At speed spray
thrown up by the wheels of the vehicle in front reduces visibility

further, and steering problems arise when ruts develop in the snow. If snow is forecast you should generally avoid towing light trailers.

Ice

Avoid towing in icy conditions. If you are unexpectedly caught in freezing conditions drive slowly, smoothly and greatly increase your following distance.

High winds

Motorways are often elevated above the surrounding countryside and tend to suffer from the effects of high winds. Be prepared for particularly strong gusts of wind on leaving cuttings, entering or emerging from under a bridge, crossing dales and going into open country. Take particular care on top of viaducts and bridges. If you anticipate high winds or sudden gusts of wind, reduce your speed to maintain stability. Regularly check your mirrors for signs of excessive trailer swing. If you observe it, ease off the accelerator to reduce the risk of snaking.

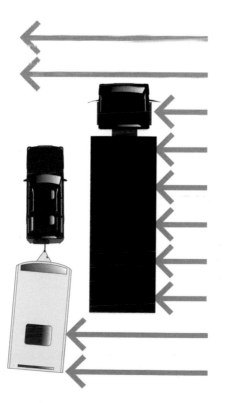

In windy conditions high-sided vehicles may suddenly veer; they also tend to act as wind breaks causing heavy buffeting to outfits as they draw past them. Reduce speed. If snaking does develop, reduce speed further and allow the steering wheel to twitch in your hands until stability is recovered.

Bright sun

Bright sunshine in the hours just after sunrise and before sunset can cause serious dazzle, especially on east/west sections of road; consider using your visors. When the sun is shining in your mirrors, adjust them to give you the best visibility with the minimum of glare. Be aware that drivers in front will have similar problems in seeing behind, and allow for this when overtaking.

Micro climates

Look out for micro climates which can cause frost and wet patches to linger in some areas after they have disappeared elsewhere. Landscape features such as valley bottoms, shaded hillsides and shaded slopes, or large areas of shadow cast by trees or buildings can cause ice to linger and result in sudden skidding. Bridge surfaces are often colder than the surrounding roads because they are exposed on all sides, and can be icy when nearby roads are not. Patchy fog is particularly dangerous and is a common catalyst of multiple pile-ups.

Ice and wetness can linger in areas of shadow.

Adapt your driving to the weather conditions. Bad weather is often blamed for causing accidents, but the real cause is inappropriate driving for the conditions that exist. In dense fog, driving at a speed at which you can stop in the distance you can see to be clear means driving so slowly that many trips are not worthwhile. The best way to deal with a skid is not to get into it in the first place. Careful observation, the correct speed, gentle use of the controls and adequate braking distances are crucial for safe driving but they are especially important in difficult weather conditions. Accidents occur when these rules are ignored.

Road surface

The type and condition of the road surface affects tyre grip and vehicle handling characteristics. Tyre grip is fundamental to driving control because it determines steering, acceleration and braking. Most drivers do not pay sufficient attention to this. Always look well ahead to identify changes in the road surface, and adjust the strength of your braking, acceleration and steering to retain adequate road holding.

Camber

Always observe the camber of the road on a curve or bend. Cambers which slope downwards to the inside of the curve help cornering. Cambers which slope upwards to the inside of the curve make cornering more difficult.

The surfaces of most roads are good for road holding when they are clean and dry. Snow, frost, ice, rain, oil, moist muddy patches, wet leaves, dry loose dust or gravel can cause tyres to lose grip. At hazards such as roundabouts or junctions, tyre deposit and diesel spillage may make the surface slippery at precisely the point where effective steering, braking and acceleration are needed to negotiate the hazard safely.

Surfacing materials	Grip characteristics	Problems
Tarmac or asphalt	Tarmac or asphalt surfaces give a good grip when they are dressed with stones or chips.	In time they become polished and lose some of their skid resistant properties.
Concrete	Concrete road surfaces often have roughened ribs which give a good skid resistant surface.	Some hold water, which freezes in cold weather and creates a slippery surface which is not easily seen.
Cobbles	Low grip when wet.	Rain increases the likelihood of skidding.

Road surface irregularities

Look out for irregularities in the road surface such as potholes, projecting manhole covers, sunken gullies and bits of debris, which can damage the tyres, suspension and coupling equipment. If you can alter your course to avoid them without endangering other traffic, do so. If you cannot, slow down to reduce shock and maintain stability as you pass over them.

The road surface in winter

In winter, the ice or frost covering on road surfaces is not always uniform. Isolated patches remain iced up when other parts have thawed out, and certain slopes are especially susceptible to this. Be on the look out for ice or frost patches, which you can detect by their appearance, by the behaviour of other vehicles and by the sudden absence of tyre noise: tyres travelling on ice make virtually no noise at all. Adjust your driving early to avoid skidding.

Driving off road

Driving off road puts the towbar, drawbar, couplings, suspension, axles and chassis of vehicle and trailer under an increased strain. Potholes, ruts, stones, lumps of concrete and masonary can, if struck by the wheels, distort and fracture any of these components. The faster you drive the greater the force of impact. Heavily or unevenly laden trailers driven over uneven ground can distort the chassis and body panels. Wheels are easily knocked out of alignment, and tyres damaged by concealed sharp objects. Off road you need to take extra care:

- keep your speed low
- if you drive through long grass, get someone to walk in front to spot concealed objects or holes
- if you get stuck in mud or on wet grass, straighten your steering and try using second gear to get moving (you do not want too much torque) – if you do get moving, keep in as high a gear as possible
- keep your revs low
- if you are stuck, consider unhitching, moving the vehicle to firm ground and using a rope to tow the trailer out of the slippery patch
- keep your speed low on tracks; they are often potholed
- 4x4s and trailers have different suspension characteristics: what feels a bit bumpy in a 4x4 might be very rough on the trailer so keep the speed low.

If despite all precautions your trailer does have a jarring experience off road, have the trailer towbar and fixing points examined by a trailer specialist.

Driving through water

Driving at speed through water can sharply deflect the front wheels and cause you to lose control. Extra care is needed at night when it is difficult to distinguish between a wet road surface and flood water. Flood water can gather quickly where the road dips and at the sides of the road in poorly drained low lying areas. Dips often occur under bridges.

As you approach a flooded area you should slow down. Avoid driving through water wherever possible. If part of the road is not flooded, use it if you can. When you have to drive through water, drive through the shallowest part but look out for hidden obstructions or subsidence.

If the road is entirely submerged, stop the outfit in a safe place and cautiously find out how deep the water is. The depth of water that you can safely drive through depends on how high your vehicle and trailer stand off the ground and where the electrical components are positioned. Consider whether your trailer is waterproof and whether water might enter the trailer, for example through the floor level vents on a caravan. Also consider whether the trailer hubs are hot, risking the suction of water into the bearings. If you decide to drive on follow the steps below.

See Chapter 2, Wheel hubs and bearings.

- Engage first gear and keep the engine running fast by slipping the clutch. This prevents water entering the exhaust pipe. In vehicles with automatic gears, use the foot brake to keep the road speed low while running the engine fast. In vehicles with manual gears, use the handbrake to control the road speed, especially when driving downhill into a ford.

- Drive through the water at a slow and even speed to avoid making a bow wave.

- When you leave the water continue driving slowly and apply the brakes lightly with the left foot until they grip. Repeat this again after a short while until you are confident that your brakes are working normally.

Night driving

Many trailer owners choose to drive at night to avoid traffic congestion, but observing in reduced light conditions is more difficult and yields less information than in full daylight. As the light dwindles your ability to see the road ahead also declines – contrast falls, colours fade and edges become indistinct.

At night your eyes need all the help you can give them. Windows, mirrors, and the lenses of lights and indicators should all be clean to give the best possible visibility. The slightest film of moisture, grease or dirt on the windows or mirrors will break up light and increase glare, making it harder to distinguish what is going on. The lights should be correctly aligned, and adjusted for the vehicle load. The bulbs should all work and the switching equipment should function properly. Trailers must be properly lit and marked at night. Windscreen washers, wipers and de-misters should also be working properly.

See Chapter 1, Lights, indicators and triangles.

Lights

On unlit roads your headlights should be on main beam unless they are dipped because of other road users.

Use dipped headlights:

● in built up areas when visibility from streetlighting is poor

● in situations when dipped headlights are more effective than the main beam, for example when going round a left-hand bend or at hump back bridge

● in heavy rain, snow and fog when the falling droplets reflect glare from headlights on full beam.

Dip your headlights to avoid dazzling oncoming drivers, the driver in front or other road users: when you overtake another vehicle, return to full beam when you are parallel with it.

You should always drive so as to be able to stop within the area that you can see to be clear; at night this is the area lit by your headlights unless there is full streetlighting. Even in the best conditions your ability to assess the speed and position of oncoming vehicles is reduced at night, so you need to allow an extra safety margin.

Dazzle

Headlights shining directly into your eyes may dazzle you. This can happen on sharp right-hand bends and steep inclines, and when the lights of oncoming vehicles are undipped or badly adjusted. The intensity of the light bleaches the retinas of your eyes and the bleaching effect can continue for some moments afterwards. During this time you can see nothing, which is clearly dangerous.

To avoid dazzle, look towards the nearside edge of the road. This enables you to keep to your course but does not tell you what is happening in the road ahead, so slow down or stop if necessary. If you are dazzled by undipped headlights, flash your own lights quickly to alert the other driver, but do not retaliate by putting on your full beam. If you did, both you and the other driver would be converging blind. If you suffer temporary blindness, stop and wait until your eyes have adjusted.

Following other vehicles at night

When you follow another vehicle, dip your headlights and allow a sufficient gap so that your lights do not dazzle the driver in front. When you overtake, move out early with your headlights still dipped. If a warning is necessary you can flash your lights instead of using the horn. When you are alongside the other vehicle return to full beam. If you are overtaken, dip your headlights when the overtaking vehicle draws alongside you and keep them dipped until they can be raised without dazzling the other driver.

Information from other vehicles' lights

You can get a great deal of useful information from the front and rear lights of other vehicles. For example, the sweep of the headlights of vehicles ahead approaching a bend can indicate the sharpness of the bend, and the brakelights of vehicles in front can give you an early warning to reduce speed.

There are other times when intelligent use of information given by lights will help your driving.

Reflective studs and markings

Reflective studs and markings are a good source of information about road layout at night. To get the most out of them you need to be familiar with the *Highway Code*. Roadside marker posts reflect your headlights and show you the direction of a curve before you can see where the actual road goes.

Cat's eyes

Cat's eyes indicate the type of white line along the centre of the road. Generally the more white paint in the line, the greater the number of cat's eyes. They are particularly helpful when it is raining at night and the glare of headlights makes it difficult to see.

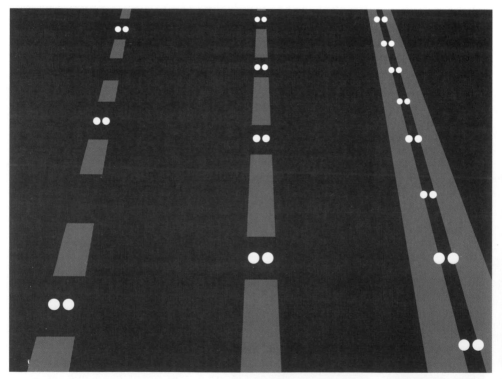

Centre lines:	Hazard lines:	Double white lines:
one cat's eye every other gap.	one cat's eye every gap.	twice as many cat's eyes as hazard lines.

Other ways to improve observation at night

● Keep your speed down when you leave brightly lit areas to allow time for your eyes to adjust to the lower level of lighting.

● Any light inside the vehicle which reflects off the windows will distract you and reduce your ability to see. In modern vehicles the dials and instruments are positioned and illuminated to avoid this but interior lights, torches, and cigarette lighters can cause reflections, so you should limit their use as much as possible.

● Certain types of spectacles – such as those with tinted lenses and those with photochromatic lenses – may be unsuitable for night driving, so check with your optician.

Night fatigue

Night driving is tiring because it puts extra strain on your eyes, and your body naturally wants to slow down as night draws on. Be aware of this problem and take appropriate action to deal with it. If you are having difficulty keeping your eyes open, you are a danger to yourself and other road users; find somewhere safe to stop, get some fresh air and rest until you are alert enough to continue safely.

See Introduction, Fatigue.

Road signs and markings

Road signs and markings provide warnings about approaching hazards, and instructions and information about road use. They need to be incorporated into your driving plan as early as possible. To make the best possible use of road signs and markings you should follow the steps below.

● Observe – actively search for road signs and markings in your observation scans, and incorporate the information they give you into your driving plan. Be particularly vigilant when you are towing for signs that warn of restricted height or lane width. Many drivers fail to see and make use of signs, and so lose valuable information.

● Understand – be able to recognise signs immediately. You should be familiar with the current edition of the *Highway Code* and the *Know your Traffic Signs* book. Everyone's memory declines over time, so check your recall of road signs and markings on a regular basis.

● React – react to a sign or marking by looking ahead to what it refers to and building the information into your driving plan. Where the sign or marking refers to an unseen hazard, anticipate the hazard and adapt your plan accordingly.

When was the last time you checked your knowledge of road signs in a current edition of the Highway Code?

Unofficial road signs

Sometimes you will see several road signs on the same pole. These should generally be read from top to bottom. The nearest event is shown by the top sign, the next nearest event by the sign below that, and so on. Always use your own observations to link the signs to the road layout ahead.

Make use of unofficial road signs such as 'Mud on Road', 'Car Boot Sale' and 'Concealed Entrance'. They provide additional information and help you anticipate the road conditions ahead.

Local road knowledge

Increasing your local knowledge of the roads can help your driving. Town driving puts heavy demands on your observation, reactions and driving skills, and you need to be alert at all times. At complicated junctions, where it is important to get into the correct lane, local knowledge is a valuable aid. But even when you know the layout of main road junctions, one-way streets, roundabouts and other local features, always plan on the basis of what you can actually see – not what usually happens. Inattentiveness is an important cause of accidents and drivers are least attentive on roads they know well. Nine out of ten accidents occur on roads that the driver is familiar with.

Making observation links

Observation links are clues to the likely behaviour of other road users. You should constantly aim to build up your own stock of observation links which will help you anticipate road and traffic conditions. Here are some examples.

When you see...	Look out for...
A cluster of lamp-posts	Probable roundabout ahead. Anticipate fuel spillages.

A single lamp-post on its own	The exit point of a junction. Anticipate fuel spillages and vehicles emerging.

No gap in a bank of trees ahead	Road curves to left or right.

When you see...	Anticipate
A coach in your mirror, moving up to overtake	Wind turbulence and suction initiating trailer swing
Railway line beside road	Road will invariably go over or under it, often with sharp turns
A row of parked vehicles	Doors opening, vehicles moving off. Pedestrians stepping out from behind vehicles. Small children hidden from view.
Ice-cream vans, mobile shops, schools buses, etc	Pedestrians, especially children.
Pedal cyclists	Inexperienced cyclists doing something erratic. Cyclist looking over shoulder with the intention of turning right. Strong winds causing wobble. Young cyclist doing something dangerous. Cyclists moving up on the nearside of your trailer.
A bus at a stop	Pedestrians crossing the road to and from the bus. Bus moving off, possibly at an angle.
Fresh mud or other deposits on road. Newly mown grass, etc.	Slow moving vehicles or animals just around the bend.
Post office vans, trades vehicles, etc.	Points where the vehicle may stop, eg post box, shops, public houses, garages, building sites, etc.
Pull-ins, petrol stations, pubs, parking places, etc	Vehicles moving in and out.
Motorway access points	Vehicles in nearside lane moving out.
Accident	Others slowing down to look.

Roadcraft video

Getting a sense of the level of observation possible for skilled drivers is difficult without instruction. One resource that goes a considerable way to illustrating the high level of road awareness possible is the *Roadcraft* video, published by The Stationery Office. This video follows police officers through an advanced driving course. It includes sections of commentary, where the officers and instructors talk about their observations as they drive, thereby providing a benchmark, which all drivers should try to meet.

Chapter 6

The system of driving control

This chapter explains a systematic approach to driving developed by the police, and shows you how to use the system to negotiate hazards. Human error is a contributory factor in nearly all road accidents. The purpose of the system is to provide a way of approaching and negotiating hazards that is methodical, safe and leaves nothing to chance – thereby significantly reducing the scope for human error.

If you use the system consistently with the right frame of mind, good observation and skill in vehicle control, you should avoid causing accidents yourself and be able to anticipate many of the hazards caused by other road users. Using the system will help to make you a calm considerate driver who is fully in control of your outfit.

Towing skills

Skilful towing requires more than pure handling skills, it also requires the right mental approach. Many driving hazards are unpredictable, and you need an investigative approach to recognise and negotiate them safely.

Driving uses both mental and physical skills:

Mental skills
The ability to scan the environment, recognise relevant dangers or hazards, decide on their priority and form an achievable driving plan.

Physical skills
The ability to translate intentions and thoughts into physical action accurately and smoothly.

When using these skills you need to take into account:

- real ability as opposed to perceived ability (what you can actually do as opposed to what you think you can do – in the average driver there is a significant gap between their real ability and their perceived ability)
- the capabilities of the outfit
- the prevailing weather and road conditions.

There is much to anticipate and think about when towing. Road and traffic conditions continually change, requiring you to adjust course and speed frequently. You need to take many factors into account: the handling characteristics of your outfit; the weight and distribution of your load; the activities of other road users, where they might be and what they might do; the closeness of other vehicles; the need to signal your intentions; the road and surface conditions; and the weather. The system of driving control simplifies this task by providing a clear and consistent method of driving.

The system of driving control gives you the essential requirement for safe towing – time to react.

Hazards

A hazard is anything that is potentially dangerous. A hazard can be immediate and obvious, such as a car approaching you on the wrong side of the road, or it may be less obvious but just as potentially dangerous, such as a blind bend which conceals a lorry reversing into your path. Much of driving skill lies in the early recognition of hazards – the situations that are potentially dangerous – and then taking the appropriate action to deal with them. One of the main causes of accidents is the failure to recognise hazardous situations – if you fail to see the potential danger you cannot act to avoid it.

See Introduction and Chapter 5

On the roads there are three main types of hazard:

- physical features such as junctions, roundabouts, bends or hill crests
- risks arising from the position or movement of other road users
- problems arising from variations in the road surface, weather conditions and visibility.

The system of driving control

The system of driving control promotes:

- careful observation
- early anticipation
- early planning
- a systematic use of the controls
- maximum vehicle stability.

It is a systematic way of dealing with an unpredictable environment and is central to *Towing Roadcraft*. It gives you the time to choose the best position, speed and gear to negotiate hazards safely and efficiently.

The five phases of the system

The system is made up of five interrelated phases:

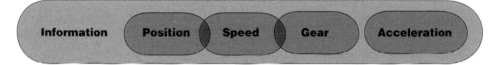

Each phase of the system depends on the one before, and you normally consider them in sequence. Start the system by considering your information needs, and then work through each phase in turn. If road conditions change, consider the new information and re-enter the system at an appropriate phase. Use the system flexibly in response to actual road conditions; do not follow the sequence rigidly if it is inappropriate to the circumstances.

Why information is so important

Taking, using and giving information is the key to the system. It starts the system and continues throughout it. You constantly need information to plan your driving and you should provide information whenever other road users could benefit from it. Because of the reduced responsiveness of an outfit, your safety depends on the early recognition and comprehension of information. Information allows you to adapt your driving to changes in road circumstances. It is the framework on which the other phases of the system – position, speed, gear, acceleration – depend.

115

Information phase: **T** take **U** use **G** give

Continuous assessment of information runs through every phase of the system.

Mirrors and signals

Constantly assess the situation ahead and to the side for changes in circumstances. Use your mirrors as often as is necessary to be fully aware of what is happening behind you. Give a signal whenever it could benefit other road users.

At certain points in the system specific checks for information are important.

Before you change course or speed you need to know what is happening in front, to the sides and behind you; mirror checks at these points are essential.

Remember the *Highway Code* advice of *mirrors – signal – manoeuvre* although you may at times decide a signal is not necessary.

Use of the horn

Sound your horn whenever you think another road user could hear and benefit from it. The purpose of the horn is to inform others that you are there. It gives you no right to proceed, and should never be used as a rebuke. It can be used at any stage of the system. Always be prepared to react to another road user's horn warning.

Consider information at every phase, especially before you change speed or direction; otherwise the system will not work.

The system of driving control

These pages set out the phases of the system

The information phase overlaps every other phase of the system.

Take information

Look all round you. Scan to the front and sides. Check your mirrors at the appropriate points in the system, and always before you change direction or speed.

Use information

Using the information you have gathered, plan how to deal with the identified hazards and make contingency plans for dealing with the unexpected. Decide on your next action using the system as a guide. If new hazards arise consider whether you need to re-run the system from an earlier phase.

Give information

If you have decided a signal could help other road users, give it; remember other road users include pedestrians and cyclists. Your options include indicators brakelights, flashing your headlights, hazard warning lights, arm signals and sounding your horn. Give a signal whenever it could benefit other road users. Generally the earlier the warning the greater the benefit.

Position yourself so that you can negotiate the hazard/s safely and smoothly. Before you change position consider checking your mirrors.

Take account of the road surface and other road users – including pedestrians, cyclists and children.

Speed

Adjust your speed to that appropriate for the hazard, taking into account visibility, the road surface, the degree of cornering required, the activities of other road users and the possibility of unseen hazards.

See Chapter 7, Acceleration; Braking; Gears; Speed

See Chapter 8, Avoiding skids

Use the accelerator, brake or, when on slippery surfaces, gears to give you the speed which will enable you to complete the manoeuvre. Make good use of acceleration sense.

Aim to make all adjustments in speed smoothly and steadily; early anticipation is essential for this.

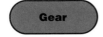

Gear

Once you have the right speed for the hazard engage the correct gear for the speed. Choose a gear that is responsive at that speed.

If you have to brake to get the right speed, you can make the gear change before the end of braking. But always avoid late braking and snatched gear changes.

See Chapter 7 Except in slippery conditions, avoid using your gears as brakes.

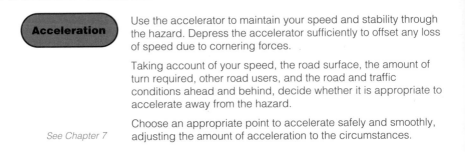

Acceleration

Use the accelerator to maintain your speed and stability through the hazard. Depress the accelerator sufficiently to offset any loss of speed due to cornering forces.

Taking account of your speed, the road surface, the amount of turn required, other road users, and the road and traffic conditions ahead and behind, decide whether it is appropriate to accelerate away from the hazard.

See Chapter 7 Choose an appropriate point to accelerate safely and smoothly, adjusting the amount of acceleration to the circumstances.

Continuous assessment of information runs through every phase of the system.

Use the system flexibly

Successful use of the system depends on how intelligently it is used. It is not an automatic mechanism but has to be adapted by you to the circumstances that arise. Used intelligently, it provides a logical but flexible sequence for dealing with hazards:

● you should consider all the phases of the system on the approach to every hazard, but you may not need to use every phase in a particular situation

● the information phase spans the whole system and entails a constant reassessment of plans

● if a new hazard arises consider whether you need to return to an earlier phase of the system.

Once you have learnt the system, practise it continually so that it becomes second nature.

The next section looks at how the system is applied to three of the commonest hazards: a right-hand turn, a left-hand turn and a roundabout.   *See Chapter 5, Planning.*

Applying the system to a right-hand turn

Acceleration

Use the accelerator to maintain your speed and stability through the hazard. Depress the accelerator sufficiently to offset any loss of speed due to cornering forces.

Choose an appropriate point to accelerate smoothly away from the hazard. Take into account your speed, the road surface, the amount of turn required, other road users, and the road and traffic conditions ahead and behind.

Gear

Once you have the right speed to negotiate the hazard, select an appropriate and responsive gear for that speed.

Speed

Adjust your speed as necessary. Use the accelerator, brake or (when necessary to avoid skidding) gears to give you the speed which will enable you to complete the manoeuvre. Make good use of acceleration sense. Know and follow the *Highway Code* advice on road junctions.

Information

Throughout this manoeuvre use your mirrors and scan to the front and sides to gather information on the position, speed and intentions of other road users. Consider giving signals or sounding your horn at any point where other road users could benefit. Remember these include pedestrians as well as cyclists, motorcyclists and drivers.

Position

Move into the appropriate position to make the manoeuvre in good time. Generally this will be towards the centre of the road, but pay attention to:

- the width and length of your trailer
- whether thre is adequate room on the nearside to accommodate the trailer and swing
- the width of the road
- any lane markings
- obstructions in the road
- the road surface and its condition
- the position, speed and size of other traffic – in front, behind and in the junction
- the flow of following traffic
- getting a good view
- making your intentions clear to other road users.

See Chapter 9

Applying the system to a left-hand turn

Always be aware of what is going on around you – make proper use of your mirrors, and shoulder checks, and always let other road users know what you intend to do. Taking, using and giving information is essential before you change speed or direction.

Information

Throughout this manoeuvre use your mirrors and scan to the front and sides to gather information on the position and intentions of other road users. Before starting the turn check carefully in your nearside mirror to make sure there are no road users 'trapped' on your nearside. Consider giving signals or sounding your horn at any point where other road users could benefit. Remember these include pedestrians as well as cyclists, motorcyclists and drivers.

See Chapter 9

Acceleration

Be aware of the possibility of cyclists and pedestrians moving up on your inside.

Use the accelerator to maintain your speed and stability through the hazard. Depress the accelerator sufficiently to offset any loss of speed due to cornering forces.

Taking account of your speed, the road surface, the amount of turn required, other road users, and the road and traffic conditions ahead and behind, decide whether it is appropriate to accelerate away from the hazard.

Choose an appropriate point to accelerate safely and smoothly, adjust the amount of acceleration to the circumstances. Do not increase speed until the whole of the outfit has completed the turn.

See Chapter 9

Gear

Select an appropriate and responsive gear for the speed at which you intend to negotiate the hazard.

Speed

Adjust your speed as necessary. Use the accelerator, brake or (when necessary to avoid skidding) gears to give you the speed which will enable you to complete the manoeuvre. Make good use of acceleration sense.

Generally a left turn is slower than a right because the turning arc is tighter. Avoid running wide as you enter the junction or you may come into conflict with other traffic, but allow sufficient room to avoid the nearside trailer wheel(s) mounting the kerb.

Position

Position towards the left of the road but pay attention to:

- the width and length of your trailer
- whether there is adequate room on the offside of your trailer to accommodate end swing without encroaching into the path of oncoming traffic
- the width of the road
- any lane markings
- obstructions in the road
- the road surface and its condition
- the position, speed and size of other traffic – both in front and behind
- the flow of following traffic
- getting a good view
- making your intentions clear to other road users.

See Chapter 9

Applying the system to approaching a roundabout

When you are on the roundabout, deal with any new hazards by using the appropriate phases of the system. Consider rear observation to both sides on exit from the roundabout.

See Chapter 9

Information

Identify hazards. Scan to the front, sides and rear. Use your mirrors before you change speed or direction. Decide early which exit to take and in which lane to approach the roundabout. Examine the road surface for anything that could reduce tyre grip: polished bitumen, oil, petrol or diesel spillages, dust and loose gravel. Be flexible, adjust your driving plan to accommodate new hazards.

Consider whether to signal.

Keep alert for an early view of traffic both on the roundabout and approaching it from other entrances.

As you approach the roundabout be prepared to stop, but look for your opportunity to go.

Acceleration

Choose an appropriate gap in the traffic to accelerate safely and smoothly onto and through the roundabout without disrupting traffic already using it. Take into account your reduced speed, extended length and increased need for space.

Gear

Select the gear to proceed onto the roundabout. This will depend on your speed the traffic conditions, your vehicle's characteristics and the load you are towing.

Speed

Lose speed smoothly, using either deceleration or brakes. Your approach speed will be determined by your view of the roundabout, the size and curvature of the roundabout and the amount of traffic using it.

Plan to stop, but look to go.

Position

Your approach position will depend on which exit you intend to take, the number of approach lanes and the lane markings. Generally if you intend to go left or straight on keep in the left lane. If you intend to turn right, approach in a lane to the right. The route through the roundabout will depend on the presence of other traffic. Always check your mirrors to make sure that no vehicles have moved up on your inside before moving across to an exit.

See Chapter 9

Chapter 7

Speed, acceleration, gears, braking and following position

Speed

The faster you drive, the more you accentuate any inherent instability in your outfit. Equally the faster you drive the more susceptible your outfit becomes to wind effects – either natural or vehicle induced – and destabilisation. Both the law and common sense require you to moderate your speed when towing – always drive at a speed that is appropriate for your outfit and the driving conditions.

See Chapter 1, Traffic law: Chapter 2, Old trailers and new vehicles.

Safety

Speed has a major impact on safety. International evidence clearly shows that lower speed limits result in fewer accidents. Drivers who drive fast regardless of the circumstances have an accident risk three to five times greater than drivers who do not. At greater speeds the risks obviously increase – you approach hazards faster, you have less time to react, and the impact damage is greater. A child hit by a car at 20 mph may be injured but will probably live: a child hit at 40 mph will probably die.

Risks increase with speed, but whatever your speed, if it is inappropriate in the circumstances, it is dangerous. This idea is central to the system of driving control. It is most clearly expressed in the safe stopping distance rule.

Drive so that you are able to stop safely on your own side of the road in the distance you can see to be clear.

This rule identifies the maximum speed at which it is safe to drive. It requires you to take account of all the circumstances before deciding the appropriate speed and to adjust your speed as circumstances alter. The capabilities of the driver, the characteristics of the outfit, and the prevailing road, traffic and , weather conditions, must all be taken into account.

The driver

As we saw in the Introduction there are both internal and external pressures which will at times encourage you to drive faster than your competence or the circumstances justify. Skilful drivers recognise these pressures and take steps to counter them.

Always drive within your competence, at a speed which is appropriate to the circumstances and the capabilities of your outfit.

As you become more experienced in towing your level of confidence may increase, but this will not necessarily make you a safer driver. You will only be safe if you also develop appropriate attitudes, recognise your own vulnerability and accurately evaluate risks.

The outfit

Different combinations have different handling characteristics. When you drive an unfamiliar outfit allow yourself time to get used to the vehicle controls and the outfit's handling characteristics before driving fast. Allow an extra safety margin until you are confident about how the outfit will respond. This is particularly important in respect of snaking.

Snaking

See Chapter 3.

Snaking describes trailer instability that develops in certain circumstances and can be extremely dangerous. The conditions in which they develop depend on weight ratios, loads and speed. It is essential that you fully understand the factors that contribute to snaking.

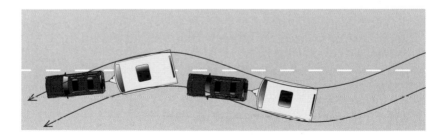

Speed limits

Statutory speed limits set the maximum permissible speed, but this is not the same thing as a safe speed. The safe speed for a particular stretch of road is determined by the actual conditions. In winter, at night, in high winds, in conditions of low visibility or high traffic volume, the statutory speed limit may well be excessive. The onus is always on the driver to select a speed appropriate for the conditions and the characteristics of the outfit.

How speed affects the driver

Vision

As you drive faster, the nearest point at which you can accurately focus moves away from you. Foreground detail becomes blurred and observation becomes more difficult because you have to process more information in less time. The only way to cope with this is to scan further ahead, so that you gain more time to assess, plan and react. In complicated situations or where there is a lot of foreground information – in a busy shopping street, for example – you need to go more slowly to observe and process the information adequately.

Statutory maximum speed limits are not the same thing as the safe speed.

See Chapter 5

Underestimating speed

It is easy to underestimate the speed at which you are riding. Speed perception is complicated and depends on several factors such as:

- the difference in detail perceived by your forward and side vision
- the engine, road and wind noise
- the unevenness of the drive
- what you regard as a normal speed
- how wide the road is and whether it is enclosed or open
- your height off the ground.

Alterations to any of these factors can alter your perception of speed. The list that follows gives some common situations where speed perception can be distorted. The solution is simple – keep a check on your speedometer.

● When you have been travelling at high speed on a motorway or other fast road and then transfer to roads where speeds below 30 or 40 mph are appropriate, these lower speeds will seem much slower than they really are. Allow time for normal speed perception to return.

● When visibility is low – in fog, sleet, heavy rain and at night – speed perceptions become distorted and it is easy to drive faster than you realise.

Check your speedometer whenever you leave a motorway or high speed road.

● When driving a vehicle that is smoother, quieter or more powerful than your usual vehicle, it is easy to drive too fast. As well as sight and balance, you use other senses to assess speed: road noise, engine noise and vibration all play a part. When one or more of these is reduced, it can seem that you are going slower than you really are.

● On wide open roads, speeds will seem slower than on small confined roads.

Speed and fatigue

Towing at speed requires a high level of attention and judgement which you cannot sustain if you are tired. Over long distances this level of concentration is itself fatiguing and you should plan adequate rest periods to recover alertness.

See Introduction

Whatever the pressures to drive faster you must always drive within your own capabilities.

Using speed safely

The skill of towing safely at speed is not easily acquired. Every driver has their own speed limit: this is the highest speed at which they are safe and comfortable in any given situation. You should know what yours is and never go beyond it. At 30 mph a minor error may be corrected but at 60 mph the same error could be disastrous.

In choosing a safe speed you must always relate the stability of your outfit to the extent of road you can see to be clear, and your ability to stop within this distance. In this respect local knowledge, if wrongly used, can be hazardous because it can tempt you to drive faster than is safe along familiar roads.

You should know the braking characteristics of your outfit and its stopping distances at different speeds. Generally assume that the stopping distances for outfits are at least 25% longer than the distances given for solo vehicles in the *Highway Code*. You should be able to apply these distances to the road you are travelling. Bear in mind that when speed is doubled braking distance quadruples, and that in wet and slippery conditions braking distances increase greatly.

Overtaking

Driving at speed may entail overtaking. Overtaking in an outfit demands careful preparation, positioning, observation and judgement of speed and distance. It is safest when carried out using the system of vehicle control combined with a full awareness of possible hazards.

See Chapter 10

Towing safely at speed depends above all else on adapting your speed to your outfit and the circumstances. The faster you go the less time you have to react and the more disastrous the possible consequences.

Key safety points

These are the key points to remember:

- the faster you go the more likely you are to experience tail swing or snaking
- drive at a speed that is safe and at which you are confident and competent
- be familiar with the controls and the handling characteristics of your vehicle – use the controls smoothly
- be familiar with the handling characteristics of your trailer and how these vary under different loads and at different speeds
- all manoeuvres take up more roadspace when towing
- towing at speed requires maximum attentiveness – if you cannot achieve a high level of attentiveness because of fatigue or some other cause, do not continue
- always drive so that you can stop within the distance you can see to be clear, by day or by night
- if you double your speed you quadruple your braking distance
- put into practice the skills developed in *Towing Roadcraft* which are designed to maximise safety

- be aware of the onset of fatigue, and take appropriate action
- no schedule is so important that it justifies an accident – it is far better to arrive late than not at all.

Acceleration

Accelerating, braking and steering are closely interrelated. They all depend for their effectiveness on the grip between the tyres and the road. As tyre grip is fundamental to these basic driving activities, you need to have a clear understanding of what it is and why it is central to your ability to control your vehicle, and the safety of yourself and other road users.

The tyre grip trade-off

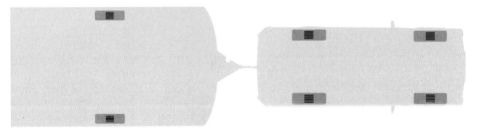

Control of your outfit is totally dependent on the grip between the tyres and the road surface.

In any given situation, there is a limited amount of tyre grip available and this is shared between accelerating, braking and steering forces. If more tyre grip is used for braking or accelerating, there is less available for steering, and vice versa.

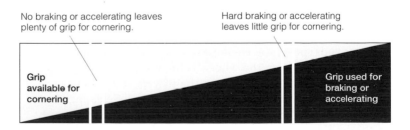

No braking or accelerating leaves plenty of grip for cornering.

Hard braking or accelerating leaves little grip for cornering.

Grip available for cornering

Grip used for braking or accelerating

Tyre grip is not necessarily the same on each wheel. It varies with the load on the wheel and this affects how the outfit handles. Braking, steering and accelerating alter the distribution of the load between the wheels and so affect the outfit's balance.

Braking or accelerating as you go round a corner or bend reduces the amount of control you have over your outfit. If more tyre grip is used for accelerating or braking, there is less available for cornering, and this reduces your control over the positioning of your outfit. Eventually, if there is not enough tyre grip for cornering, a skid will develop. The more slippery the road surface, the earlier this will happen. The exact outcome depends on the balance of the outfit, and the relative efficiency of the brakes on the trailer and on the towing vehicle.

The more you brake or accelerate, the less your ability to corner.

Braking going down hill on a bend is particularly hazardous. As more tyre grip is used up in braking, the tyre grip available to keep the outfit on course round the bend diminishes. If the braking is sharp, there is a real risk of a heavily laden unbraked trailer jack-knifing and swinging round to the inside of the bend, and of a braked trailer skidding round to the outside of the bend. It is best to avoid braking at all in these circumstances, but if it must be done, the brakes should be applied very gently and smoothly. The safest course would be to reduce speed before the hill and to select a low gear to control speed; any braking should be confined to straight sections of road.

unbraked trailer

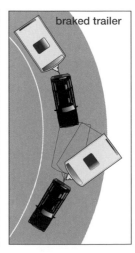
braked trailer

Sharp braking on a bend going down a hill risks the trailer swinging out of control.

Using the accelerator

Providing you are in the right gear, depressing the accelerator will increase the outfit's speed. If you are in a gear that is too high for your speed, the engine will not be able to respond because the load from the wheels is too great. Changing to a lower gear reduces the load from the wheels and the engine is able to speed up and so move the outfit faster. Selecting the correct gear is of great importance in towing. The extra weight of the trailer reduces the range over which gears are able to be responsive, and requires more precise matching of gear to road speed.

When the accelerator pedal is released, the opposite effect – deceleration – occurs. The engine speed slows down and cylinder compression slows the vehicle, and therefore the outfit, down. The lower the gear the greater the slowing effect of the engine (because there are more compression strokes for each rotation of the wheels).

So, in the appropriate gear, the accelerator pedal has two effects:

● **increase in speed** when the pedal is depressed

● **decrease in speed** when the pedal is released.

Acceleration and vehicle balance

Acceleration alters the distribution of weight between the wheels of the vehicle. When a vehicle accelerates the weight is lifted from the front and pushed down on the back wheels. This alters the relative grip of the front and rear tyres. During deceleration the opposite happens.

During acceleration   During deceleration

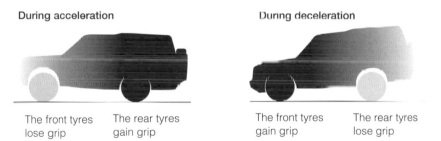

The front tyres lose grip   The rear tyres gain grip   The front tyres gain grip   The rear tyres lose grip

With a braked trailer in tow, the loss of rear tyre grip under deceleration (braking) is reduced by the transfer of weight from the trailer onto the rear of the towing vehicle. The precise effect depends on the trailer's posture, whether it is braked and how its load is distributed – you need to observe the precise effect in practice. But as weight is transferred to the towing vehicle it is removed from the trailer tyres, reducing their grip on the road.

Developing your skill at using the accelerator

Jerky acceleration is uncomfortable for the passengers, puts unnecessary strains on the vehicle and trailer, and adversely affects tyre grip throughout the outfit. Use the accelerator deftly, making precise and smooth movements to depress or release it.

Acceleration capability varies widely between vehicles and depends on the size of the engine, its efficiency and the power-to-weight ratio. Take time to become familiar with the acceleration capability of any vehicle you drive: the safety of many manoeuvres, particularly overtaking, depends on your good judgement of it.

Always consider the safety implications of accelerating. Sudden sharp movements of the accelerator reduce tyre grip and jeopardise steering control. The faster you go the further you will travel before you can react to a hazard. It will take you longer to stop and, if you crash, your impact speed will be higher.

Acceleration sense

Acceleration sense is the ability to vary vehicle speed in response to changing road and traffic conditions by accurate use of the accelerator. It is used in every driving situation: moving off, overtaking, complying with speed limits, following other vehicles and negotiating hazards. Good acceleration sense requires careful observation, full anticipation, sound judgement of speed and distance, driving experience and an awareness of your outfit's characteristics. A lack of acceleration sense causes many common mistakes: for example, accelerating hard away from a junction and then having to brake sharply to slow to the speed of the vehicles in front; or accelerating to move up behind a slower moving vehicle and then having to brake before overtaking. If you have good acceleration sense you are able to avoid unnecessary braking.

Accelerating on bends

A moving vehicle and trailer are at their most stable when they are evenly balanced, the vehicle is just pulling without increasing road speed, and they are travelling in a straight line. Accelerating to increase the road speed round a bend upsets these conditions.

If you accelerate hard and alter direction at the same time you run the risk of demanding too much from the available tyre grip. If the tyres lose grip you lose directional control. To get maximum directional control, avoid altering your road speed at the same time.

As soon as an outfit turns into a bend it starts to slow down and lose stability, due to cornering forces. If you maintain the same accelerator setting as you go into and round a bend you will lose road speed.

To maintain constant speed round the bend and retain stability you need to increase power by depressing the accelerator. How much to depress the accelerator is a matter of judgement but **your purpose is to maintain constant speed, not to increase it.** Increasing road speed on corners reduces vehicle stability.

When you need to steer and increase speed together, use the accelerator gently. Use extra care in slippery conditions or you will get wheel spin, loss of steering control and a skid.

Acceleration reduces the ability to corner because it shifts the vehicle's weight on to the back wheels and reduces front tyre grip. In all vehicles this increases the risk of front wheel spin and loss of steering control, but in vehicles with front wheel drive the risk is accentuated because the front wheels are the driving wheels. Do not make the mistake of applying even more steering which may lead to an eventual loss of control.

3

Coming out of the bend

As the road begins to straighten and you start to return to the upright, start to accelerate smoothly.

2

Entering the bend

While the curvature of the bend is constant, open the throttle sufficiently to maintain a constant speed round the bend.

1

Approaching the bend

As you approach the bend, assess the road surface and adjust your speed so that you can stop in the distance you can see to be clear on your own side of the road.

The key points to remember are:

- set your speed for a bend according to the overall stopping distance
- maintain a constant speed round the bend
- the harder you accelerate, the less your steering ability
- use the accelerator smoothly – jerkiness causes tyre slip
- watch out for slippery surface conditions, and adjust your speed.

Gears

The way you use your gears can make or mar your towing. Skilful use of the gears depends on accurately matching the gear to the road speed, and using the clutch and accelerator precisely. Your vehicle can only increase speed if the engine can deliver the power. It can only do this if you are in the right gear. You should aim to:

- be in the correct gear for every road speed and traffic situation
- make all gear changes smoothly
- engage a chosen gear without going through an intermediate gear first
- know the approximate speed range for each gear when towing.

It is useful to understand how the gears work as this will help you get the most out of them. The main effect of the gears is to transform speed of turning into power of turning and vice versa.

- The bottom gear produces plenty of power but relatively little speed.
- The top gear produces plenty of speed but at relatively low power.

The gears in between produce varying combinations of power and speed. To climb a steep hill or pull a heavy load the road wheels need plenty of power, which is gained at the expense of speed by selecting a low gear. Cruising on a level stretch of motorway requires speed but relatively little power: speed is gained at the expense of power by selecting a high gear.

To gain speed quickly, select a lower gear. This has more power to drive the outfit along faster. This is because the engine can only increase its speed if the load on it is not too great. A lower gear supplies more power to the wheels and so reduces the load on the engine. But the top speed of a lower gear is limited and eventually you have to change to a higher gear to gain more speed: turning power is converted into speed of rotation.

The greater turning power of low gears also affects tyre grip. The higher the turning power, the more likely tyre slip becomes. This is why it is advisable to use a higher gear when moving slowly in slippery conditions such as on snow, ice or mud. It is also why tyre slip occurs when you accelerate hard in first gear.

Moving off from stationary

The ideal way to move off from a standing start is to accelerate smoothly and to gather speed by steadily working up through the gears. Overaccelerating in low gears or remaining in a gear beyond the limits of its optimum performance damages the engine, uses excessive fuel and results in slower progress. Some engines cut out or misfire if excessively revved and this could be dangerous.

Key pointers to skilful gear use

- Recognise when to change gear by the sound of the engine.

- Choose the right gear for the load and speed: often when towing this is a lower gear than usual.

- Use the brakes rather than engine compression to slow the vehicle (except during hill descents and when there is a risk of skidding).

- Brake in good time to slow to the right road speed as you approach a hazard, and then select the appropriate gear.

- Match your engine speed to road speed by keeping the accelerator depressed when you change down. This will avoid any jerkiness as the clutch engages.

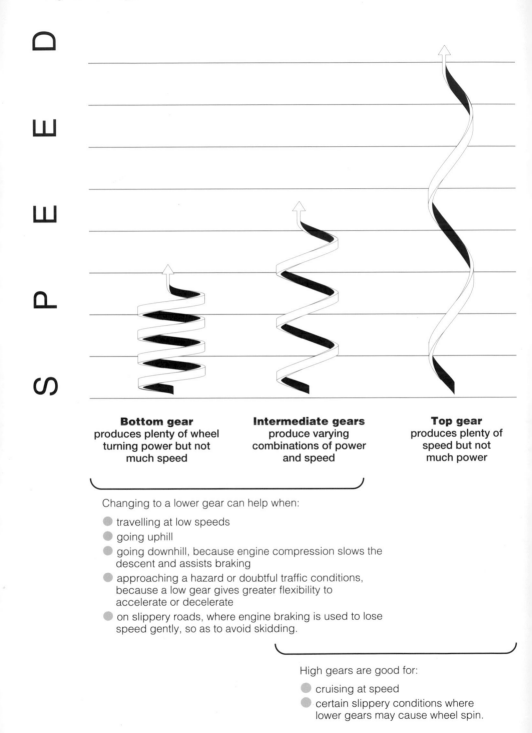

SPEED

Bottom gear
produces plenty of wheel turning power but not much speed

Intermediate gears
produce varying combinations of power and speed

Top gear
produces plenty of speed but not much power

Changing to a lower gear can help when:

- travelling at low speeds
- going uphill
- going downhill, because engine compression slows the descent and assists braking
- approaching a hazard or doubtful traffic conditions, because a low gear gives greater flexibility to accelerate or decelerate
- on slippery roads, where engine braking is used to lose speed gently, so as to avoid skidding.

High gears are good for:

- cruising at speed
- certain slippery conditions where lower gears may cause wheel spin.

Braking

You need to be able to slow down or stop your outfit with it fully under control. The smoothness of a drive is greatly improved by early anticipation of the need to slow down or stop, and by braking gently and progressively. The ability to accurately estimate the required braking distance at different speeds and with different loads is a central skill of safe towing. There are two ways of slowing down or stopping:

- decelerating (releasing the accelerator pedal)
- using the brakes.

Deceleration

When you release the accelerator the engine slows and through engine compression exerts a retarding force on the wheels. This causes the engine to act as a brake, reducing road speed smoothly and gradually with little wear to the vehicle.

The loss of road speed is greater when you decelerate in a low gear. (This applies equally to automatic gearboxes.) Deceleration, or engine braking, provides a valuable way of losing speed on slippery roads. If the accelerator is released gently, it provides a steady and smooth braking effect in conditions where normal braking might lock the wheels or send the trailer into uncontrollable snaking. Engine braking is also useful on long descents in hilly country, but for normal driving it is inadequate for more than gradual variations in speed.

Braking

Use the brakes if you need to make more than a gradual adjustment in road speed. You should generally keep both hands on the wheel while you brake, and plan to avoid braking on bends and corners. You can apply pressure to the footbrake to achieve the slightest check, or until all the wheels lock up (or, where fitted, the automatic braking system intervenes). Always check the effectiveness of the brakes in the outfits you drive, and make allowances for extra loads or changes in road surface. If the brakes on your trailer appear to be weak or snatch, have them checked immediately.

Testing your brakes

Every time you use your outfit check that the brakes are working. Check them when the vehicle is stationary before you move off, and check them again when the outfit is moving.

The stationary test

- Check that the brake pedal moves freely and gives a firm positive pressure. Check that the vehicle handbrake fully brakes the wheels.

- With the vehicle and trailer coupled, fully apply the trailer handbrake. Try to move forward in first gear – movement should be minimal or not at all. Next try to reverse – trailers fitted with standard brakes should be reluctant to move, those with auto-reverse brakes should move a little and then become reluctant to move further. If the trailer fails either test have it checked.

- With the trailer uncoupled and the handbrake fully applied, compress the coupling head. It should move smoothly into the housing. When it is fully depressed, release it and it should run out smoothly. If it is very resistant to compression or does not move out smoothly, have it checked.

The moving test

- Soon after moving off, select a straight stretch of road where it is safe to do the test. Ensure that there are no vehicles following close behind. Brake normally. If the coupling bangs or snatches or the trailer weaves sharply, have the brakes checked. You only need to do this test once a day, provided you have no reason to suspect the performance of the brakes. Always consider the safety and convenience of other road users before you do a moving test.

Normal braking

Braking should normally be progressive and increased steadily.

| Gerntly take up the initial free movement of the pedal | Increase the pressure progressively as required | Relax pedal pressure as unwanted road speed is lost | relax the pedal just before stopping to avoid a jerking halt |

Braking, tyre grip and balance

Braking reduces the ability to steer because of its combined effects on tyre grip and outfit balance. On a bend this reduces stability and can cause the vehicle's back wheels to lock and go into a rear wheel skid. The harsher the braking, the greater the tyre slip and the less the ability to steer. In slippery conditions harsh breaking almost inevitably results in a skid. Research by the Caravan Club has shown that for most drivers ABS significantly reduces outfit braking distances because it allows maximum braking effort to be applied, regardless of skill.

The safe stopping distance rule

This guiding principle of *Towing Roadcraft* should always be observed. It relates the distance you can see to be clear to the shortest distance you can stop in and therefore your speed. It enables you to assess whether your speed is safe in any situation.

Never drive so fast that you cannot stop comfortably on your own side of the road within the distance you can see to be clear.

The importance of this rule for your own and other people's safety cannot be overstated. It provides a guide to the speed at which you should corner, and it indicates the speed and distance you should keep from other vehicles in all other traffic conditions. Successfully applying this rule requires skill. You need to be aware of:

- the braking capabilities of your outfit
- the type and condition of the road surface – in slippery or wet conditions braking distances increase greatly
- the effects of cornering, braking and outfit balance on tyre grip.

The only variation to this rule occurs in narrow and single track lanes where you need to allow *twice* the overall stopping distance that you can see to be clear. This is to allow sufficient room for any oncoming vehicle to brake also.

Overall safe stopping distance

As the *Highway Code* explains the safe stopping distance is made up of two parts:

Thinking distance + Braking distance = Stopping distance

- **Thinking distance** is the distance travelled in the time between first observing the need for action and acting. The average driver reacts to expected events in 0.7 seconds. The distance covered in that time is the same figure in feet as the speed in miles per hour; for example, at 30 miles per hour thinking distance is 30 feet.

Actual thinking distance varies according to the speed of the vehicle, your physical and mental condition, your attentiveness and whether or not you are expecting something to happen. Drivers take much longer to react to unexpected events than to expected ones.

● **Braking distance** is the distance needed for braking in dry conditions. It depends on the vehicle's capability, the trailer's capability, the gradient of the road and the condition of the road surface. Rising or falling gradients have a significant effect on deceleration and braking distances. Slippery surfaces greatly increase braking distances.

The distances given in the *Highway Code* are the shortest stopping distances in good conditions for a solo vehicle. These distances should be increased by at least 25% for outfits, and then doubled again for wet weather and multiplied ten times for icy or snowy conditions. If the vehicle behind you is too close, drop back further from the vehicle in front. This will allow you to brake more gently in an emergency and may prevent you being rammed from behind.

Braking on corners and bends

Because braking affects the balance, stability and cornering ability of your outfit, special care is needed when braking on a corner or bend:

● generally plan to avoid braking on corners because it reduces your ability to steer and induces trailer swing; if braking is necessary, apply the brakes gently and steadily

● brake in plenty of time

● adjust brake pressure according to the condition or grip of the road surface

● on steep winding descents, keep your speed low. Brake if possible only on the straight stretches and if necessary only very gently on the bends. Use a low gear at an early stage in the descent.

Following position

Following too closely to the vehicle in front is one of the main causes of accidents. This is as true on slow-moving urban roads as on motorways. Increasing your following distance is probably the single most effective thing you could do to reduce your accident risk.

In a stream of traffic, always keep a safe distance behind the vehicle in front. A guide for following distances in open conditions is 1.25 metres per mph between your outfit and the vehicle in front. Use the stopping distances given in the *Highway Code* as a guide, but increase them by 25% to allow for the additional weight of your trailer. On single carriageways, a minimum following distance of 100m is recommended to allow faster vehicles to overtake you.

The two-second rule

On fast roads, the standard advice when you are driving solo in good conditions is to leave at least a gap of two seconds between you and the vehicle in front. Again this gap needs increasing for outfits – use a gap of three seconds. One easy way to count this additional time is to alter the standard rhyme so that it now reads:

Only a fool breaks the two-second rule.
If you tow that's too low

This time should be at least doubled in wet weather and increased by ten times in icy conditions. If the vehicle behind you is too close, drop back further from the vehicle in front. This will allow you to brake more gently in an emergency and may prevent you being rammed from behind.

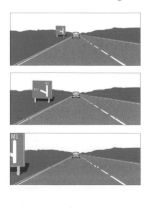

Note when the car in front passes a convenient landmark.

Count one second

Count two seconds
If you pass the object before you have counted three seconds, you are too close. Drop back and try the test again.

Always try to maintain a view of the road beyond the vehicles you are following. Below are some of the advantages of keeping your distance from the vehicle in front:

- you have a good view, and can increase it along both sides by slight changes of position – this enables you to be fully aware of what is happening on the road ahead
- you can stop your outfit safely if the driver in front brakes firmly unexpectedly
- you can extend your braking distance so that the driver behind has more time to react
- you suffer less from the spray from the vehicle in front in wet weather
- you can see when it is safe to move up into the overtaking position.

In this illustration the driver is following too closely to the vehicle in front. The aerial plan shows how hazards in the shaded area cannot be seen.

In this illustration the driver is keeping a good safe position and all the hazards are visible. This view could be improved by moving slightly to the nearside or offside.

Chapter 8

Steering, reversing, cornering and avoiding skids

This chapter looks at practical skills for manoeuvring an outfit safely, especially when reversing and cornering, at how to avoid skids and what to do if you feel a skid developing.

Steering

A correctly loaded, well-matched, well-maintained outfit should hold its course along a flat, straight road with minimal steering. Camber, crossfall, or side winds can move the outfit to one side but a small steering adjustment will compensate for this and keep it on a straight course. Usually you only need to make positive steering adjustments when you alter course or turn the outfit.

Different combinations of vehicle and trailer have different handling characteristics, so take time to become familiar with the different steering characteristics of each combination you drive.

Steering technique

The tried and tested police technique of pull–push steering is well suited to towing. This method keeps both hands on the wheel for most of the time and gives firm control and efficient steering in a wide range of circumstances.

Seat position

Good steering starts with getting your body in the right position in relation to the steering wheel. Before you start your engine, adjust the position and angle of your seat so that you can reach the controls comfortably. Also make sure you have a good view through your mirrors along both side of the outfit – adjust your mirrors if necessary. You should aim for a position which allows greatest control of the steering without being uncomfortable. An uncomfortable position causes fatigue and detracts from your driving.

141

How to hold the steering wheel

- Place your hands on the wheel with your palms on the rim at about the quarter-to-three or ten-to-two position.

- Fold your fingers round the rim and your thumbs along it.

- Hold the wheel lightly but be ready to tighten your grip if necessary.

- Keep both hands on the wheel while you are driving unless it is necessary to give an arm signal or to operate a control. Always keep at least one hand on the wheel.

This hold enables you to turn the wheel immediately in either direction. Make changes in direction smoothly and gradually. Make small changes in direction by turning the steering wheel without altering your hand hold.

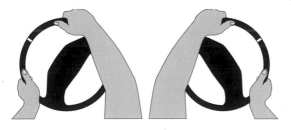

To make more positive turns, use the pull–push method described below.

Pull–push

With the pull–push method neither hand passes the twelve o'clock position. Your hands remain parallel to each other on the steering wheel except when you move a hand up for the initial pull or when you make small alterations in course. One hand grips and makes the turn, the other slides round its side of the wheel ready to continue the turn. The advantage of pull–push is that it keeps both hands on the wheel and allows an immediate turn in either direction at any point during steering.

The explanation of the pull–push method given below is for a left-hand turn. For a right-hand turn follow the same method but replace left with right, and vice versa.

● Start the turn with a pull and not a push because it gives better control.

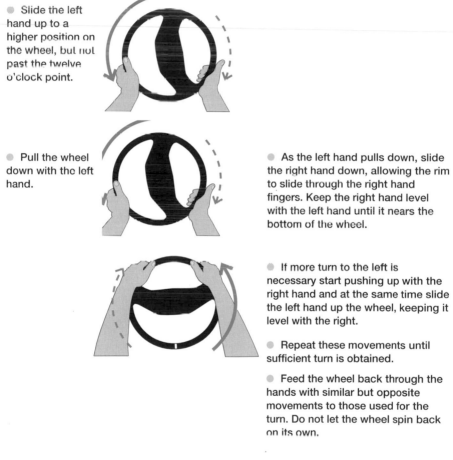

● Slide the left hand up to a higher position on the wheel, but not past the twelve o'clock point.

● Pull the wheel down with the left hand.

● As the left hand pulls down, slide the right hand down, allowing the rim to slide through the right hand fingers. Keep the right hand level with the left hand until it nears the bottom of the wheel.

● If more turn to the left is necessary start pushing up with the right hand and at the same time slide the left hand up the wheel, keeping it level with the right.

● Repeat these movements until sufficient turn is obtained.

● Feed the wheel back through the hands with similar but opposite movements to those used for the turn. Do not let the wheel spin back on its own.

Manoeuvring at slow speeds and in confined spaces

Manoeuvring in a confined space sometimes requires rapid movements of the steering wheel. Generally the standard pull–push technique provides effective steering, but on occasions, especially when reversing, other hand holds may give better control.

Avoid the temptation to turn the steering wheel while the vehicle is stationary. It damages the tyres and puts excessive strain on the steering linkages, particularly in vehicles with power assisted steering. Only turn the steering wheel when the vehicle is moving, even if it is only moving very slowly.

Steering guidelines

These are the key points to remember for effective steering:

- do not place your elbows on the window frame or arm rests because this reduces control

- place your hands on the wheel in the ten-to-two or quarter-to-three position: only grip tightly when you need to exert maximum effort

- keep both hands on the wheel when cornering, braking firmly or driving through deep surface water

- on slippery roads steer as delicately as possible or you may skid.

Good steering requires good observation, anticipation and planning. If the brakes are applied sharply or if the speed is too high, steering cannot be precise.

Reversing

Learning to reverse an outfit is something of a knack. The key to gaining the knack is first to understand what you need to do, secondly to do everything very slowly and gently, thirdly to make early and small adjustments, and finally to find a large safe space in which to practise. When learning, it is easiest to tackle reversing in a straight line first, then to deal with reversing round a corner.

Safety
If you have a large trailer, it is safest to get someone to help you to reverse because there is inevitably an area behind your trailer which you cannot see. Never reverse without checking that there is not a person, animal or obstacle behind the trailer. If you have no assistant, get out of the vehicle and check the blindspot yourself.

Reversing brake

If you have a pre-1989 trailer which does not have auto-reverse brakes, do not forget to use the reversing lever to manually disengage the brakes. After completing the manoeuvre you must re-engage the brakes by releasing the reversing lever. With auto-reverse brakes do not forget to pull forward slightly after reversing to re-engage the handbrake mechanism.

Reversing hold

Put one hand at the top of the steering wheel and use this hand to move the wheel. Use the other hand to hold the wheel low down, either loosely while the wheel slides through or tightly when you take a new grip at the top. Look in your mirrors and over your shoulders to get a clear view. You can improve your view to the left by putting your left arm on the back of the seat. If the seat belt restricts your movement, release it but do not forget to put it back on if you intend to continue towing.

Reversing in a straight line

- Pull forward to get your vehicle and trailer in a straight line, with an equal amount of trailer showing in your left and right mirrors.

- Carry out safety checks.

- Move backwards gradually, checking your mirrors all the time.

  As more of the trailer becomes visible in one mirror...

 gradually turn your steering wheel towards that mirror to re-align the trailer.

  The aim is to keep equal amounts of trailer visible in each of the mirrors.

Reversing round a corner

It is easiest to reverse round an offside corner because you can look out of the window to see where your trailer is. Do not forget that the front of your vehicle will swing first to the inside and then to the outside of the curve as you reverse.

- Pull forward to get your vehicle and trailer in a straight line, with an equal amount of trailer showing in your left and right mirrors. Position yourself so that you are about a trailer's length from your intended entry, and with sufficient roadspace to allow the towing vehicle to swing from side to side.

- Carry out safety checks.

- Start the turn by turning your steering wheel to the opposite side to that which you intend to reverse. If you find this confusing try the 'Australian method' – hold the steering wheel in the 6 o'clock position and turn it to the side you want to go. This first turn of the steering wheel sets the vehicle at the right angle to the trailer for the turn.

- When the trailer starts to turn, gradually rotate the steering wheel in the opposite direction to the intial steer you put on the wheel; ie turn the top of the wheel towards the side that you want to reverse. This guides the whole combination round the bend. As you reverse, constantly check in your mirrors and adjust the steering wheel to get the exact curve you want.

- Do everything gradually so that you do not jack-knife. If you do, or you oversteer, pull forward, check for safety and start again. If your vehicle is at the correct curvature to the trailer you will not have to restart with the opposite lock.

The 'Australian method'

Hold the steering wheel in the 6 o'clock position

then turn it to the side you want to go.

This first turn of the steering wheel sets the vehicle at the right angle to the trailer for the turn.

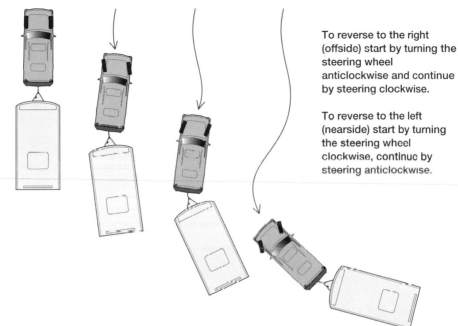

To reverse to the right (offside) start by turning the steering wheel anticlockwise and continue by steering clockwise.

To reverse to the left (nearside) start by turning the steering wheel clockwise, continue by steering anticlockwise.

Advice on reversing

Reversing can be difficult, especially in confined areas. The faster it is done the more difficult it is to control, so always reverse slowly. Before you reverse:

● scan the area for suitability and obstructions

● ensure you have an unobstructed view

● get someone to help you if possible.

While reversing:

● move slowly and slip the clutch if necessary – in automatic vehicles you can control the speed by using the left foot on the brake

● remember that as you reverse an outfit round a corner, the front of your vehicle moves first to one side then to the other, and could strike nearby objects or come into conflict with other road users

● look all round you to make sure there are no hazards.

If your reversing lights fail use your indicator lights or brakelights to light the area behind you when it is dark, but be careful not to mislead other road users.

Cornering

Developing skill at cornering

Cornering is one of the commonest driving activities, and it is important to get it right. When you corner your outfit loses stability, and you place extra demands on the tyre grip available. The faster you go and the tighter the bend, the greater these demands are.

This section sets out the general principles of cornering, the forces involved, factors affecting your ability to corner safely and the limit point technique for assessing the correct speed.

Using the system of driving control for cornering

Because cornering is potentially dangerous, we need clear guidelines on how to corner safely. The system of driving control provides these guidelines.

Guidelines for safe cornering

Information
Gather information on the severity of the bend, the position and speed of other road users and the condition of the road surface as you approach the bend.

Position
Place your outfit in the right position for the bend on the approach.

Speed
Get the right speed for the corner or bend before you enter it. You must be able to stop on your own side of the road in the distance you can see to be clear.

Gear
Select the right gear for the speed before you enter the bend.

Acceleration
Set your accelerator to sustain the correct speed round the bend.

Applying these guidelines requires good judgement and planning. But before we look in more detail at using the system of driving control for cornering, it is helpful to consider the other key factors that affect an outfit's ability to corner.

Cornering forces

A moving outfit is at its most stable when travelling in a straight line on a level course and at constant speed. It will continue to travel on a straight course unless some other force is applied to alter its direction. When you steer, the turning force to alter direction comes from the action of the towing vehicle's front tyres on the road. This force depends on tyre grip. If the front tyre grip is broken, the outfit will continue in a straight line. If the trailer tyres lose grip the outfit will either oversteer, or spin out of control. On tighter bends, at higher speeds and with heavier loads, the demands on tyre grip are greater.

(As you corner, your body feels as if it is being pushed out towards the side of the vehicle. In fact it is continuing to move in a straight line and only turns into the bend because it is forced to by the vehicle.)

Tyre grip faces competing demands from three forces:

- steering
- accelerating
- braking.

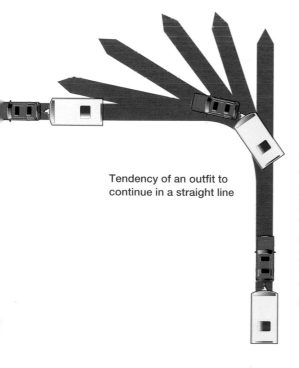

Tendency of an outfit to continue in a straight line

The more you brake or accelerate the less tyre grip you have for steering. The faster you go into a corner or bend, the greater the tyre grip required to keep your outfit on course.

The practical outcome of these forces is that when tyre grip is lost, vehicle and trailer continue in a straight line, separately or together, rather than turning. So in a left-hand bend, as tyre grip is lost, your outfit or trailer moves to the right of your intended course; and in a right-hand bend your outfit or trailer moves to the left. The characteristics of the outfit will reduce or accentuate these tendencies.

Outfit characteristics

Outfits vary in their ability to corner; they only corner well if they are:

● well-matched

● hitched at the correct height

● correctly loaded and balanced, with the correct noseweight

● well-maintained – steering, suspension, shock absorbers, tyres and overrun brakes all affect the outfit's balance and road grip when cornering. The correct tyre pressures in all the outfit's tyres are critical to stability.

Vehicle specification

The specifications of the towing vehicle affect the outfit's handling characteristics:

● the type of drive (front wheel, rear wheel or four wheel)

● the condition and type of suspension and damping

● whether ABS is fitted

● whether traction control is fitted

● whether adaptive suspension is fitted

See Chapter 2

● the drive ratio and central differential characteristics on a four wheel drive vehicle.

Camber and superelevation

The road surface is not normally level across its width but is built with a slope to assist drainage. The slope across the road affects steering. The normal slope falls from the crown of the road to the edges and is called camber.

● **On a left-hand bend** camber increases the steering effect because the road slopes down in the direction of turn.

● **On a right-hand bend** camber reduces the steering effect because the road slopes away from the direction of turn.

(This only applies if you keep to your own side of the road. If you cross over the crown to the other side of the road, camber will have the opposite effect on steering.)

There are many instances, especially at junctions, where the slope across the road surface is at an unexpected angle.

Whatever the slope, if it falls in the direction of your turn it will increase the effect of your steering; if it rises in the direction of your turn it will reduce the effect of your steering. You need to consider the slope across the road when deciding on your speed for a bend.

Superelevation is where the whole width of the road is banked up towards the outside edge of the bend, making the slope favourable for cornering in both directions.

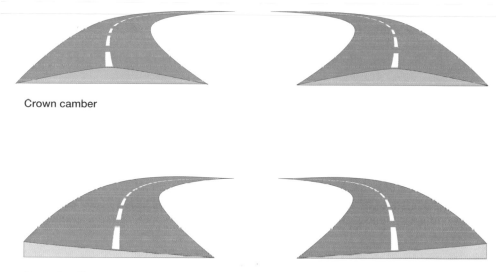

Crown camber

Superelevation

Summary of factors affecting cornering

To sum up, the factors that determine your outfit's ability to corner are:

- speed
- the amount of steering you apply
- the amount of acceleration and/or braking
- the characteristics of the outfit and its loading ·
- the slope across the road surface – camber and superelevation
- the road surface and how the weather has affected its grip.

The limit point

The limit point is a very useful aid in assessing the severity of a bend and the correct speed for going round it. Use it together with the other observational skills developed in Chapter 5 and the system for an effective and safe method of cornering.

As you approach a bend using the system you should be seeking as much information as possible about the severity of the bend. You should use all the observational aids and clues available to you (weather, road surface, road signs, road markings, the line made by lamp-posts and trees, the speed and position of oncoming traffic, the angle of headlights at night, etc) to anticipate and plan for the curvature of the bend. The limit point assists observation because it provides a systematic way of judging the correct speed through the bend.

What is the limit point?

The limit point is the furthest point along a road to which you have an uninterrupted view of the road surface. On a level stretch of road this will be where the right-hand side of the road appears to intersect with the left-hand side of the road. This point of intersection is known as the limit point. To tow safely you must be able to stop on your own side of the road within the distance you can see to be clear – that is, the distance between you and the limit point.

The ability to stop on your own side of the road in the distance you can see to be clear determines how fast you can go.

Approaching the bend

- At first the limit point appears to remain at the same point in the road. Reduce your speed to be able to stop safely within the remaining distance.

- As you approach the bend take information about the sharpness of the bend and carefully assess the appropriate speed for cornering.

1

2

3

Going through the bend

- Just before you enter the bend the limit point begins to move round at a constant speed. Adjust your speed and gear, if necessary, to the speed of this movement.

- You now have the correct speed and gear for the bend. Select the gear to match the speed *before* entering the bend.

Coming out of the bend

- As the bend starts to straighten, your view begins to extend and the limit point starts to move away more quickly. As your steering straightens out accelerate towards the limit point.

- As the bend comes to an end, continue to accelerate to catch the limit point until other considerations such as speed limits or new hazards restrict your acceleration.

4

5

6

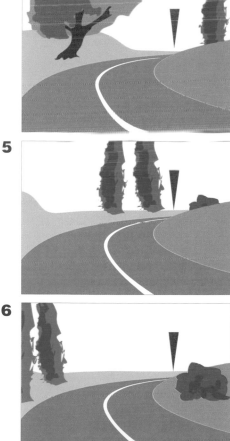

7

8

9

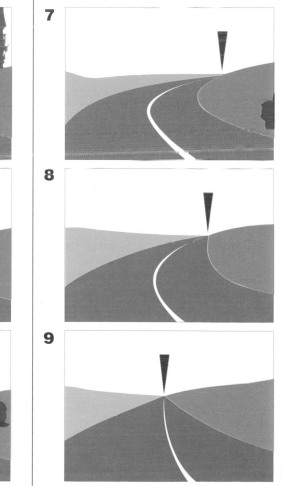

The more distant the limit point the faster you can go because you have more space to stop in. The closer the limit point the slower you must go because you have less space to stop in.

Match your speed to the speed at which the limit point moves away from you providing you can stop within the distance you can see to be clear.

As you approach and go through a bend the limit point appears at first to remain stationary, then to move away at a constant speed and finally to sprint away to the horizon as you come out of the bend. The technique of limit point analysis is to match your speed to the speed at which the limit point appears to move. If it is moving away from you, accelerate. If it is coming closer to you or standing still, decelerate or brake. Even if the bend is not constant, you can still match your speed to the apparent movement of the limit point, because this will vary with the curvature of the bend.

The advantages of using the limit point together with the system are:

- it ensures that you observe the driving safety rule of matching your speed to your ability to stop within the distance you can see to be clear

- it gives you the appropriate speed to approach and negotiate bends

- it gives you the appropriate speed to go round a bend, and therefore the appropriate gear to be in

- it gives the point at which to start accelerating

- it is self-adjusting: as road visibility and conditions deteriorate you have less distance or ability to stop, and so your speed must be reduced to compensate.

Using the system for cornering

This section takes you through the five phases of the system identifying key considerations at each phase and explaining how to use limit point analysis in the speed phase. As with any other use of the system, you should work through it methodically, selecting the phases that are appropriate.

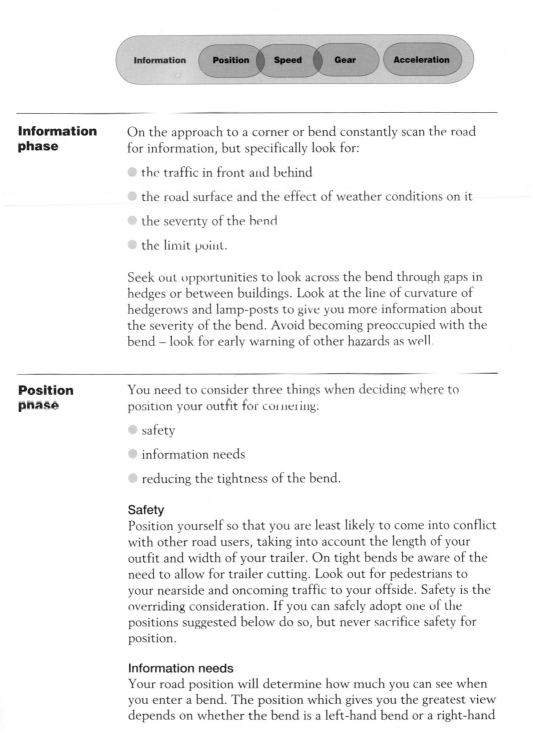

Information phase

On the approach to a corner or bend constantly scan the road for information, but specifically look for:

- the traffic in front and behind
- the road surface and the effect of weather conditions on it
- the severity of the bend
- the limit point.

Seek out opportunities to look across the bend through gaps in hedges or between buildings. Look at the line of curvature of hedgerows and lamp-posts to give you more information about the severity of the bend. Avoid becoming preoccupied with the bend – look for early warning of other hazards as well.

Position phase

You need to consider three things when deciding where to position your outfit for cornering:

- safety
- information needs
- reducing the tightness of the bend.

Safety

Position yourself so that you are least likely to come into conflict with other road users, taking into account the length of your outfit and width of your trailer. On tight bends be aware of the need to allow for trailer cutting. Look out for pedestrians to your nearside and oncoming traffic to your offside. Safety is the overriding consideration. If you can safely adopt one of the positions suggested below do so, but never sacrifice safety for position.

Information needs

Your road position will determine how much you can see when you enter a bend. The position which gives you the greatest view depends on whether the bend is a left-hand bend or a right-hand bend. For a right bend the best viewing position is towards the nearside and for a left bend it is towards the offside. But always put safety first.

Reducing the tightness of the bend

The other thing to consider is reducing the tightness of the curve through which you drive. By moving your outfit from one side of the available road space to the other you can follow a shallower curve and thereby improve stability. The path you take is different for a right- or a left-hand bend, but always consider safety first. Do not take a straighter course unless you can see fully ahead. Often you will not be able to do this until the road begins to straighten out.

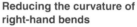

Reducing the curvature of right-hand bends
If you have a view across a bend and there is no oncoming traffic, take a gradually curving path towards the centre of the road. Allow enough space on the offside for the trailer cutting the corner (trailer cutting). Then ease the outfit back towards a more normal position on the other side of the bend. Under no circumstances must any other road users be endangered. Look at the diagram to the left and you can see that the curve made by the outfit following this course is straighter than the curve of the bend itself.

Reducing the curvature of left-hand bends
Keep towards the centre line until you can see clearly ahead. Then drive your outfit through a gradual curved path towards the nearside of the road, allow ample space on the nearside for trailer cutting. Moving into a more normal position on the other side of the bend.

Position – right-hand bends

Position yourself as far to the left as possible to allow for trailer cutting on your offside. Be wary of parked vehicles and pedestrians and give them sufficient clearance. Other dangers to consider are blind junctions or exits, adverse cambers and poor condition of the nearside road surface. Keep to the left until you can see all the way round the bend. Before assuming a more central position as you come out of the bend, check that no vehicles are taking the opportunity to try and overtake you.

Position – left-hand bends

Position yourself towards to the centre line but only as far as necessary to allow for trailer cutting on the left. This will also improve your view. Before you adopt this position consider:

- approaching traffic and other offside dangers which require more space for safety

- whether your position might cause other road users to think you intend to turn right, and who might then attempt to pass you on the nearside.

Speed phase

When you have adopted an appropriate position, the next phase of the system is to consider and obtain the appropriate speed to enter the bend.

Use the limit point to judge the safe speed to drive round the bend. Where the curve round the bend is constant, the limit point moves away from you at a constant speed. This gives you the speed for the bend unless the curvature changes. If the bend tightens, the limit point appears to move closer to you, and you should adjust your speed accordingly to remain within the safe stopping distance.

In assessing the speed to go round a bend, you need to consider:

- your outfit's characteristics

- the road and road surface conditions

- the traffic conditions

- the weather conditions.

When you assess the situation, do not think, 'What is the fastest that I can go round this bend?' but rather, 'Can I stop in the distance I can see to be clear?' – that is, just before the limit point.

Gear phase
When you have achieved the right speed, and before entering the bend, engage the appropriate gear for that speed. Select the gear that gives you greatest flexibility and will enable you to accelerate appropriately on the far side of the bend. The condition of the road surface needs to be included in these considerations: in wet or slippery conditions, harsh acceleration in a low gear may well result in wheel spin and the loss of steering control.

Acceleration phase
Depress the accelerator sufficiently to maintain a stable speed round the bend. Providing there are no additional hazards, start to accelerate when the limit point begins to move away and you begin to straighten your steering. (Check that no vehicles are attempting to overtake you first.)

As you continue to straighten your steering, increase your acceleration to 'catch' the limit point. Accelerate until you reach the speed limit or other considerations, such as the stability of your outfit, restrict your speed.

Avoiding skids

Avoiding skids is of critical importance when towing because of the difficulty of regaining control of an outfit once a skid develops. Because of this, the advice in this section concentrates on skid avoidance.

Vehicle features which reduce the risk of skidding

Antilock braking systems (ABS) and traction control systems are increasingly fitted to vehicles, and help to reduce the risk of skidding. While they do reduce the risk of the towing vehicle losing tyre grip, they cannot be relied on to wholly prevent skidding, even in the towing vehicle. But as they only operate on the towing vehicle, the trailer remains fully exposed to the risk of skidding. Providing their limitations are recognised, they are a worthwhile addition to towing safety.

Vehicles fitted with these features behave differently from other vehicles, and require different driving techniques. It is essential to read and understand the manufacturer's guidance on how to use them.

Antilock braking systems (ABS)

The purpose of an ABS is to retain the ability to steer during harsh or emergency braking.

ABS monitors the speed at which each wheel is rotating and compares it with pre-programmed data. The system senses the slowing down of the wheels during braking and is programmed to release the brakes before the wheels fully lock up. It reapplies the brakes once the wheels start to turn again. In principle the wheels should never lock, but on a slippery surface the wheels may not rotate immediately the braking pressure is released, allowing momentary lock-up.

Once the system is activated, the driver is required to maintain maximum pressure on the brake pedal, only releasing it when the need for braking has passed.

ABS does no more than provide the driver with an additional safety device. It does not increase the grip of the tyres on the road, nor can it prevent skidding. In limited circumstances a vehicle equipped with ABS can stop within a shorter distance than if the wheels were locked, but it does not reduce, and could increase, the stopping distance on a slippery surface. If you activate the antilock braking system, this suggests that you are not driving within safe limits.

Traction control systems

Traction control improves steering and vehicle stability by controlling excess wheel slip on individual wheels. It reduces engine power when there is excessive wheel slip, allowing the wheels to regain traction (or grip) and stability. It allows the vehicle to make maximum use of tyre grip, especially on slippery surfaces and where the friction of the road surface is uneven (for example, where one wheel is on a normal surface and the other on mud, snow or ice).

The technique of skid control is fundamentally different in a vehicle fitted with traction control. Different manufacturers use different systems of traction control, so **if your vehicle has traction control you must consult your vehicle handbook and follow the manufacturer's advice on what to do in skid situations.**

Avoiding skidding

What causes a skid? Many people when asked this question would say that it was the result of poor road or weather conditions, but this is not really true. A skid does not just happen – it is almost always the result of a driver's actions. It is usually caused by altering course or speed too harshly for the road conditions.

Your aim should be to drive your outfit in a way that ensures it does not skid. This becomes more difficult when road or weather conditions deteriorate. In such conditions your skills of observation, anticipation and planning can do a lot to minimise the risks of skidding. But as the weather deteriorates there will come a point when no responsible driver should take a trailer out.

How does a skid happen?

A skid occurs when one or more tyres lose their normal grip on the road, causing an unintended movement of the vehicle, trailer or both. This happens when the grip of tyres on the road becomes less than the forces acting on the outfit. The forces that operate on an outfit are:

- accelerating forces
- braking forces
- cornering forces.

These forces act whenever you operate the vehicle controls – the brake, the accelerator, the clutch or the steering wheel. If you brake or accelerate while steering round a bend or corner, two forces are combined. As we saw in Chapter 7, there is only limited tyre grip available and if these forces become too powerful they break the grip of the tyres on the road. Never drive to the limits of the tyre grip available – always leave a safety margin to allow for the unforeseen.

Skidding is usually the result of driving too fast for the conditions. If a driver suddenly or forcibly accelerates, brakes, releases the clutch without matching engine speed to road speed or changes direction, this may cause wheel spin. On a slippery road surface, it takes much less force to break the grip of the tyres. Drivers who tow high-sided trailers must also take into account wind-effects, either natural or man-made, as a force that makes demands on the tyre grip. Again, speed is relevant.

The faster you go the more susceptible your outfit is to the effects of buffeting, suction and wind.

If you have ever experienced a skid, you will probably remember that you were changing either the speed or direction of the vehicle – or both – just before the skid developed.

Causes of skidding

The commonest causes of skidding are:

- excessive speed for the circumstances
- coarse steering in relation to a speed which is not itself excessive
- harsh acceleration
- sudden or excessive braking
- snatching brakes.

If you feel a skid developing you should try and remove the cause:

- ease off the accelerator if you are accelerating
- ease off the brakes if you are braking (except for ABS vehicles)
- ease off the steering and accelerator if you are cornering.

If you start to skid – remove the cause.

Minimising the risks of skidding

Use your understanding of the causes of skidding together with the skills of observation, anticipation and planning to reduce the risks of skidding.

Observe –
weather and road conditions to watch out for

Skidding is more likely in bad weather conditions and on slippery road surfaces. These are some of the obvious and less obvious hazards you need to watch out for:

- rain
- snow, ice, frost – you should ask yourself whether you are being responsible in towing at all in these conditions
- wet mud, damp leaves, oil or diesel which can create sudden slippery patches on the road surface

- cold spots in shaded areas, under trees, on slopes or hills – watch how other vehicles behave in icy weather

- dry loose dust or gravel

- a shower or rain after a long dry spell – accumulated rubber dust and oil mixed with water can create a very slippery surface

- worn road surfaces that have become polished smooth

- concrete, which usually provides good grip, but which may hold surface water and become slippery in freezing weather

- cobbled roads, still found in some towns and cities, which become very slippery when wet

- changes in the road surface on bridges, which may be more slippery than the surrounding roads.

The risk of these hazards is accentuated at corners and junctions because you are more likely to combine braking, accelerating and steering in these situations.

Anticipate and plan – adjust your driving to the road conditions. Good road observation will enable you to evaluate poor weather and road conditions accurately and adjust your speed accordingly.

- Leave plenty of room for manoeuvring, reduce your speed and increase the distance you allow for stopping to match the road conditions – on a slippery surface an outfit can take many times the normal distance to stop.

- Use a higher gear in slippery conditions to avoid wheel spin, especially when moving off or travelling at low speeds.

- On a slippery surface aim to brake, steer and change gear as smoothly as possible, so that the grip of the tyres is not broken. Smooth gear changes are important so as not to activate the trailer's override braking mechanism.

Care of the outfit

Most skids are the result of inappropriate driving technique, but keeping your outfit in good condition is also important in minimising the risk of skidding:

- tyres must be correctly inflated and have adequate tread depth – check tyre treads and tyre pressure regularly

- defective brakes and faulty suspension are especially dangerous on slippery surfaces and may help to cause or aggravate a skid –

do not increase the risk by neglecting these problems

● the overrun and braking mechanism on the trailer must be in good working order to prevent snatching and to provide smooth progressive braking.

Recognising and removing the cause of a skid

If your outfit gets into a full skid, you are unlikely to have the time or space to correct it. You need to be able to recognise different types of skid in the early stages in order to respond quickly and regain grip between the tyres and the road. When you feel a skid developing, your first action is to remove the cause.

Cause	How to remove the cause

speed or acceleration which is excessive for the road surface

Many skids are caused in this way. At higher speeds you need more tyre grip to corner or stop. When surface grip is low, altering speed or direction can exceed the available grip, causing a skid. The faster you go the more likely this becomes. Harsh acceleration can also cause the wheels to spin, even at low speeds.

● One method is to remove pressure from the accelerator and steer to correct the direction of the outfit. In most cases releasing the accelerator will be sufficient to prevent the skid developing further.

● Another method is to depress the clutch to remove the drive from the road wheels, and to steer to correct the direction of the outfit. Release the accelerator and keep the clutch pedal depressed until it is safe to re-engage the drive. Re-engage the drive smoothly because any sudden jerkiness can restart the skid. Use the accelerator to exactly match the engine speed to the road speed and release the clutch very smoothly.

Do not declutch in vehicles fitted with traction control because it does not operate when the clutch is depressed.

Cause	How to remove the cause

excessive or sudden braking

Some skids are caused by braking too harshly for the road conditions – often because of a sudden hazard such as a child running into the road. Excessive braking causes a skid because the tyres lose their grip and the wheels lock up.

Most people's instinctive reaction to a sudden hazard is to brake hard. If a skid then develops the usual response is to want to brake even harder. Learning to overcome this reaction in vehicles not fitted with ABS is crucial.

● Relaxing pressure on the brake allows the wheels to rotate, restoring tyre to road surface grip and some directional control. (Do not do this in vehicles fitted with ABS but keep the brakes applied and steer.)

coarse steering

Steering too sharply for the speed of the outfit increases one of the forces that can break the grip of the tyres on the road. An outfit uses least tyre grip when travelling in a straight line. As soon as you start to corner you place extra demands on the tyre grip. If you steer too sharply for the speed you will break the tyre grip and go into a skid. You can go round the same bend, at the same speed, in the same conditions and lose control by steering harshly instead of smoothly. You should aim to make your steering as smooth as possible.

● Reduce speed immediately by either removing pressure on the accelerator or declutching (do not declutch in a vehicle fitted with traction control). This allows the tyres to regain grip on the road, thereby restoring directional control. Steer in the direction you wish to go.

Aquaplaning

One of the most frightening experiences a driver can encounter is aquaplaning. This is where a wedge of water builds up between the front tyres and the road surface, often because of an inadequate depth of tyre tread. Whether you brake or steer the outfit will not respond. The safest solution is to remove pressure from the accelerator or to declutch, allowing the outfit to lose speed and the tyres to regain their grip. Do not turn the steering wheel while aquaplaning because the towing vehicle will lurch whichever way the wheels are pointing when the tyres regain grip.

Key pointers for avoiding skids

● Do not tow if road conditions are likely to be slippery

● only drive an outfit which is well-matched, well maintained, correctly loaded and balanced, and has the correct noseweight

● drive at an approriate speed for the conditions

● steer, brake, accelerate and change gear smoothly

● if you feel a skid developing, remove the cause.

Chapter 9

Junctions and other hazards

This chapter deals with everyday hazards that you encounter on the road: junctions, roundabouts and hills. It raises key observational points which you should incorporate into your driving plan as you approach the hazards using the system of driving control.

Junctions

Turning into or out of a junction on the left is problematic because of the restricted roadspace available for the turn. Care must always be taken to avoid mounting the nearside kerb with the trailer wheels. On right-hand turns, although there is more roadspace available for the manoeuvre, there is the additional problem of crossing the path of oncoming traffic. Below we deal with each of these manoeuvres in turn.

Left-hand turns into a side road

● Well before the turn, take a central position to allow for trailer cutting and to get a better viewpoint. Always be aware of the need to position so as to avoid conflict with oncoming traffic.

● As you get closer to the junction, continually assess it. Reposition yourself to the left if the curvature of the kerb is of the gradual half-moon type.

● If the turn is tight, consider whether the trailer end swing will conflict with oncoming traffic. If it will, wait for a suitable break in the traffic flow before starting the turn.

● Throughout the manoeuvre, be alert to the possibility of cyclists creeping up on your nearside.

Left-hand turns out of a side road

● Take a central position on the approach to the junction.

● When assessing an adequate gap in the traffic on the main road, remember that your outfit is longer and slower than a solo vehicle.

● When turning into a narrow two-way road, make sure there is an adequate gap in the traffic on both sides of the road if there is any chance that part of your outfit might cross the central line.

● At the junction take a sweep which is wide enough to prevent the trailer wheel(s) hitting the offside kerb. Remember that your trailer will take a tighter path than your vehicle because of trailer cutting.

● Avoid turning into the junction so late that you stray unnecessarily over the central line.

Right-hand turns into a side road

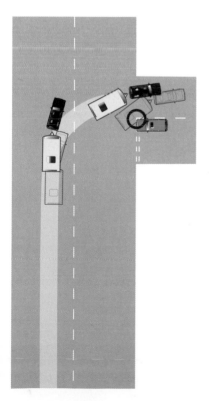

● On the approach, position to the left but only so far as to allow for trailer cutting should the junction be tight. Also be aware of the need for sufficient space on the nearside to allow for trailer end swing.

● Be alert to the possibility that positioning too far to the left might encourage following vehicles to attempt to overtake on your offside. Early indicating will help to reduce this problem but always check in your mirrors before you start turning.

● At the junction, position your vehicle further forward for the turn than you would normally to allow for trailer cutting, and to avoid hitting any vehicle waiting to turn out of the side road.

● Wait for a gap in the oncoming traffic that takes into account the length of your outfit and the time it takes to manoeuvre. Check your offside mirror to make sure no one is attempting to overtake before starting to turn.

- Steer your vehicle close to the nearside kerb of the side road, but do not mount the kerb. As you straighten up, position your vehicle in the centre of your side of the road.

- Your trailer will follow a tighter curve than your vehicle but should avoid cutting the corner.

Right-hand turns out of a side road

- Take a normal position on the approach to the junction.

- If the turn is tight, allow sufficient room on the nearside to accommodate trailer end swing.

- When assessing an adequate gap in the traffic on the main road remember that your outfit is longer and slower than a solo vehicle.

Other entrances and exits require essentially the same positioning but be alert to the presence of gateposts on the inside of the turn with all trailers and on the outside of the turn with wide trailers.

Crossing dual carriageways

Extra care needs to be taken when crossing dual carriageways. You must assess whether the central reservation is deep enough to accommodate the whole length of your outfit. If it is, treat each carriageway as a separate road, waiting in the central reservation after crossing the first carriageway for a suitable gap in the traffic on the second. If the central reservation is not deep enough to accommodate the whole of your outfit, you must wait until you can cross both carriageways in one go. You must not block part of the first carriageway with your trailer while waiting for a gap in the traffic on the second. To do so is very dangerous.

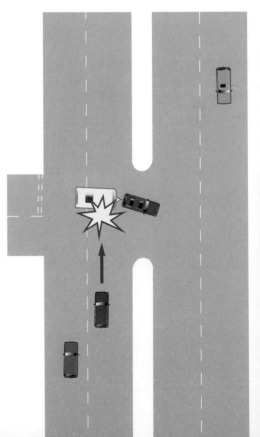

Roundabouts

Outfits require additional space and time to negotiate a roundabout. Make allowances for this in assessing a suitable gap to pull onto the roundabout. Care needs to be taken to give the trailer sufficient space on the offside so that it does not mount the island, and on the nearside so that it does not mount the exit kerb. A careful mirror check needs to be made to make sure that nothing is trapped on the nearside as you move over to leave the roundabout.

● Approach the roundabout in the left lane for left and straight on; keep in the left lane round the roundabout. Leave sufficient space on your nearside to avoid clipping the kerb as you enter and leave the roundabout.

● Approach in a right lane for right exits; take a course towards the centre of the roundabout allowing sufficient space on the offside for trailer cutting. After passing the exit before the one you want, check mirrors, indicate and move over towards your exit. Be alert to the possibility of trapping vehicles on your nearside. Allow sufficient space on the nearside as you leave to avoid the trailer wheel(s) clipping the kerb.

See Chapter 6

● On mini-roundabouts use all the roadspace available on the nearside. If it is unavoidable that the trailer wheel clips the island, drive slowly.

Hills and gradients

Hills present a number of difficulties for outfits. The maximum towing weight for a car is determined by the weight it can tow from a standing start on a 12% (1:8) incline. Attempting to restart with a full load on hills steeper than 12% exceeds the design limits of the car. Hills steeper than 25% (1:4) are just too steep for most outfits whether moving or not. Another important consideration to bear in mind is that the overrun brakes do not prevent the trailer running backwards when the outfit is facing uphill.

When planning a journey in hilly country use a map which is detailed enough to give an indication of steep gradients. Plan your routes to avoid them.

Towing uphill

- Remember the additional weight of your outfit and select a lower gear on the approach to the hill. Keep up the revs to maintain progress.

- If you need to stop on a hill, apply the handbrake before releasing the footbrake. Gradually release the footbrake to see whether the handbrake will hold the outfit. If it will not, depress the footbrake. You will have to heel and toe the footbrake and accelerator to move off. Hold the footbrake on with one half of your right foot while you use the other half to depress the accelerator to get sufficient revs to release the clutch. Once moving, slide the whole of your foot onto the accelerator.

- Another technique which eases starting on a hill is jack-knifing the outfit. If there is enough room and it is safe to do so let your outfit roll back, turning the steering to jack-knife the outfit. Then when you move off, you will be driving across the slope, and have the opportunity to get the outfit moving before having to bear the full weight.

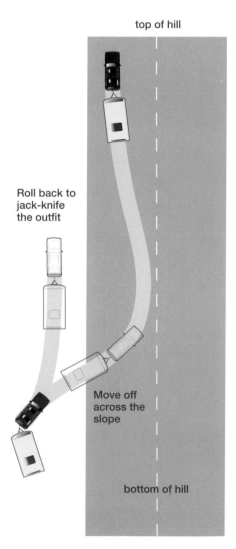

top of hill

Roll back to jack-knife the outfit

Move off across the slope

bottom of hill

Towing downhill

- On the approach to the hill observe any gradient signs, reduce your speed and select an appropriate low gear. Reduce the speed further if there are any indications that the hill has a slippery road surface, strong crosswinds or is used by large, fast, high-sided vehicles.

- If you have to further reduce your speed while going downhill, try to brake on the straight sections of road and not on the bends. It is important that all braking is smoothly applied.

- Remember that brakes applied during a long descent are likely to fade. Use engine braking – by selecting a low gear – instead.

- Keep your speed low when going downhill to maintain stability. There is an increased risk of snaking while going downhill because of the change in the dynamics of the outfit – the trailer pushing rather than the towing vehicle pulling. If you are driving too fast downhill and some external force (wind, buffeting, bumps in the road surface) sets up a sideways force your trailer may start snaking.

- If you are going downhill – but only when going downhill – and your trailer starts snaking you may have to brake very lightly to recover from the snake. Anything but the smoothest of braking will make the situation worse.

Chapter10

Overtaking and being overtaken

Overtaking with a trailer in tow

Overtaking while towing is hazardous because of the increased length of the outfit and the reduced ability to accelerate. It will take more time, and require much more road space than when driving solo. You need an extensive gap in the oncoming traffic to complete it safely. There are many hazards to consider when overtaking: the system of driving control will help you carry out the manoeuvre safely.

Remember that overtaking is your decision and you can reconsider it at any point.

Key safety points

When considering whether to overtake, always follow this safety advice:

● do not overestimate your ability to accelerate, nor underestimate the length of your outfit

● do not overtake where you cannot see far enough ahead to be sure it is safe; this is particularly important where hill crests or corners could conceal fast moving vehicles

● avoid causing other vehicles (overtaken, following or approaching) to alter course or speed

● always be able to move back to the nearside in plenty of time

● always be ready to abandon overtaking if a new hazard comes into view

● do not overtake in situations where you might come into conflict with other road users (these are identified in the overtaking section of the *Highway Code*)

● never overtake on the nearside on dual carriageways except in slow-moving queues of traffic when offside queues are moving more slowly.

Overtaking places you in a zone of potential danger, and requires good judgement if it is to be safe. The ability to overtake with consistent safety only comes with experience and practice. Even when you have acquired this skill you need to be extremely cautious. Always be patient and leave a margin of safety to allow for errors. If in doubt hold back.

Passing stationary vehicles

Overtaking stationary vehicles is relatively straightforward. Use the system to approach and assess the hazard, and to pass it with safety. Take account of the position and speed of oncoming traffic, the position and speed of following traffic and the presence of pedestrians. If the situation allows, keep at least a door's width away from the side of the stationary vehicle.

Overtaking moving vehicles

Overtaking a moving vehicle is more complicated because the hazards are moving and the situation changes all the time. You need to consider the speed, length and acceleration capabilities of your outfit, and the relative speeds of other vehicles. You also need to be able to predict where vehicles and gaps in the traffic will converge. To do this safely requires careful observation and planning, good judgement of speed and distance, and an awareness of the many possible secondary hazards.

How to overtake

When you are catching up with another vehicle you should decide whether to adjust your speed and follow while it makes reasonable progress, or to overtake at the first safe opportunity. Whatever your decision, careful use of acceleration sense will assist the ease and smoothness of your manoeuvre. If you decide to overtake, assess whether you can approach and overtake in one continuous manoeuvre, or whether you will have to follow for a while until a suitable opportunity arises. Either way, the vehicle in front is a hazard so you need to consider the various phases of the system to deal with it safely.

You will meet other road users besides vehicles, and you need to consider their special needs. Avoid startling horses. Be aware that cyclists, especially children, can be erratic and allow them plenty of room. Give motorcycles good clearance and be aware that if you are too close your slip stream could destabilise them.

The three-stage technique for overtaking

This technique describes how to overtake a vehicle which you have been following. The three-stage approach is illustrated in the diagram.

Stage 3
overtaking

Stage 2
tho overtaking position

Stage 1
tho following position

Stage one: the following position

Where you are gaining on a vehicle in front, and it is not possible to overtake immediately, use the system of car control to reduce your speed to that of the vehicle in front to follow at a safe distance.

Your main task in the following position is to observe and assess the road and traffic conditions for an opportunity to overtake safely. You need to ask yourself the questions below:

Have you taken into account the speed, acceleration, length and manoeuvrability of your outfit?

What is the speed and length of the vehicle to be overtaken?

What distance does your outfit need to overtake and regain a nearside gap safely?

Is there a possibility of as yet unseen vehicles approaching at high speed?

Is it sensible to try to overtake the vehicle in front?

What will be the likely response of the driver and occupants of the vehicle in front?

What is happening behind: are any of the drivers behind likely to overtake you?

What is the speed of approaching vehicles in view?

Does the road layout present a hazard?

Observe what is happening in the far distance, the middle ground, the immediate foreground and behind; do this repeatedly and check your mirrors frequently.

Your safety depends on making the correct interpretation of what you see. It is not enough just to see it.

In some circumstances it may be possible, as you close up on a vehicle in front, to miss out stage one and go straight to stage two: the overtaking position. This is determined by your view of the road ahead and whether any additional hazards are present that would make the overtaking position unsafe. If you do go straight to the overtaking position you still need to observe and assess the hazards identified in the diagram.

Stage two: the overtaking position

The overtaking position is closer than the following position and minimises the distance you have to travel to overtake. It can also indicate to the driver in front that you wish to overtake. Adopt this position so that you are ready to overtake when a safe opportunity arises.

Because it is closer than the following position you have less time to react to the actions of the vehicle in front, so you must be sure that there are no hazards ahead which might cause it to brake suddenly. You can only know this if you have been able to fully observe the road ahead.

Work through the stages of the system to move up to the overtaking position.

Information
Observe the road ahead and behind for an opportunity to safely occupy the overtaking position. Take into account hazards that can be seen and the possible dangers in areas that cannot be seen. Plan your move when you see an opportunity developing. Consider the need to signal.

Position
Move up to the overtaking position. This is the closest position to the vehicle in front that is consistent with the hazards and that gives an adequate view of the road ahead. It is not possible to define this position exactly, it depends on an awareness of the possible dangers, good judgement and experience. The larger the vehicle in front, the further back you need to be. Also be aware that the closer you get to the vehicle in front the more likely you are to intimidate the driver.

Speed
Adjust your speed to that of the vehicle in front.

Gear
If you are not already in an appropriate gear, select the most

When following a large vehicle take a view along both sides of the vehicle.

responsive gear for the speed, bearing in mind that this is the gear you will use to accelerate as you overtake.

As the overtaking position is closer than the following position you must observe carefully for any new hazards. If a hazard comes into sight consider dropping back to the following position until the hazard is passed. When planning to overtake you need to know exactly what is on the road ahead and behind, and to be aware of the possible pitfalls. Observation, planning, judgement of speed and distance and attention to detail are crucial. Thoughtless overtaking is dangerous.

Stage three: overtaking

From the overtaking position continue observing until you identify an opportunity to overtake, then re-run the system of car control to guide you while overtaking.

Information

Identify:

- a safe stretch of road along which you have adequate vision

- the speed of any approaching vehicles

- the relative speed of your outfit and the vehicle(s) you intend to overtake

- a gap in the approaching traffic which gives you sufficient time to complete the manoeuvre

- a gap in the traffic on your side into which you can safely return

- what is happening behind.

Consider the need to give information: is the driver in front aware of your presence, do you need to signal your intentions to the driver behind? Consider the benefits of giving a headlight, horn or indicator signal.

Position

Having made a thorough information check and decided it is safe to go, recheck your mirrors, particularly for any vehicle attempting to overtake you, give any necessary signals, and move out deliberately but without swerving to an offside position. Generally, do this without accelerating. From this new position make a thorough information check of the road ahead and behind for any unidentified hazards. Decide whether to continue with overtaking.

Speed

Overtake if the situation is clear, accelerating if necessary. If you are overtaking a high sided vehicle anticipate some buffeting and tail swing. While you are in the offside position you are in a zone of potential danger so move through it as briskly as possible.

Gear

Before moving out to overtake you should have selected a suitable gear for the manoeuvre. Sometimes circumstances may require another gear change, but you should generally avoid changing gear during overtaking itself. Keep both hands on the steering wheel throughout the whole manoeuvre if possible.

Acceleration

Adjust your speed to complete the overtaking manoeuvre safely, and to enter the gap you have identified. Move into the gap smoothly and without swerving. Use the accelerator to adjust your speed if possible.

Summary of the overtaking manoeuvre described in stage three

1 Position yourself to obtain the best view.
2 If in doubt, hold back.

3 Overtake.

4 Move back to the nearside in plenty of time.

Special hazards to consider before attempting to overtake

We have just worked through the three-stage technique for overtaking systematically. But to present it as clearly as possible we did not include important aspects of road and traffic conditions which must be considered before overtaking. These are essential to safety, and are explored next.

The *Highway Code* has a section which gives advice on overtaking. The illustrations below show some common accident situations that can arise if this advice is not followed.

The driver of the white outfit does not realise that the driver of the blue car can see only the slow-moving bus and may move out into the path of the overtaking car	The driver of the white outfit fails to foresee that the blue car may turn without warning into a side road, cutting across the path of the overtaking outfit	The driver of the white outfit fails to appreciate that the driver of the blue car is looking only to the right and may pull out as the overtaking car approaches on the wrong side of the road	The driver of the white outfit fails to appreciate that the lorry is not indicating to overtake the car ahead, but is turning right

The range of hazards you must consider

Before overtaking you must consider the full range of possible hazards that each situation presents:

- the vehicle in front
- the vehicle behind
- the road layout and conditions
- overtaking in a stream of vehicles
- overtaking on bends
- overtaking on a single carriageway
- overtaking on a dual carriageway
- overtaking downhill.

Each of these is discussed below.

The vehicle in front

Assess what sort of hazard the vehicle in front presents.

- Has the driver of the vehicle noticed you?
- Can you predict from earlier behaviour whether the response of the driver is likely to be aggressive?
- Does the size or the load of the vehicle prevent the driver from seeing you or prevent you from seeing the road ahead clearly?
- Is it a high-sided vehicle?

Make your intention to overtake clear to the driver in front. Your road position and following distance help you to do this, but take care not to appear intimidating. This could provoke an aggressive response in the other driver who might speed up as you try to overtake. If the driver in front appears to be obstructive, consider the implications. Firstly, is it worthwhile overtaking at all and secondly, how much extra speed and space do you need to allow for this?

If the driver in front has not noticed your presence or has loads which obscure the rear view mirrors, take this into account. Consider the use of the headlights or horn to inform the driver of your presence.

Take extra care before overtaking a long vehicle. The combined length of your outfit and the long vehicle will require you to be in the offside for a considerable time and distance. If appropriate, take views to both sides of the vehicle and ensure that there is ample space to overtake and return safely to your own side. The same applies to vehicles that have wide or high loads: be sure that you have observed carefully and are aware of any possible dangers in the road ahead.

If the vehicle you intend to overtake is high-sided be prepared for wind tubulence and buffeting. Anticipate the effect of this on your trailer. Hold the steering wheel firmly, but allow it to twitch in response to tail swing.

The vehicle behind

Assess whether the vehicles behind pose a risk. When an opportunity to overtake becomes available to you, it is often available to the vehicles following you as well. Note their speed, position and progress, and judge whether they may attempt to overtake you. Be aware that other vehicles may come forward from behind the vehicle behind you. Consider the need to signal your intentions. Use your mirrors to monitor the situation behind you, especially before changing your speed or position.

Road layout and conditions

When planning to overtake, consider the layout of the road ahead very carefully. Look for nearside obstructions or junctions (including pathways, tracks, entrances, farm gates) out of which vehicles or other hazards could emerge, and cause the vehicle(s) you intend to overtake suddenly to veer to the offside. On the offside, look carefully for junctions, especially where they could conceal emerging vehicles or other hazards.

Look for lay-bys on both sides of the road and be alert to the possibility that a vehicle might pull out of them. Be especially attentive to offside lay-bys. Drivers leaving them may not see you because they are concentrating on what is happening behind rather than in front of them.

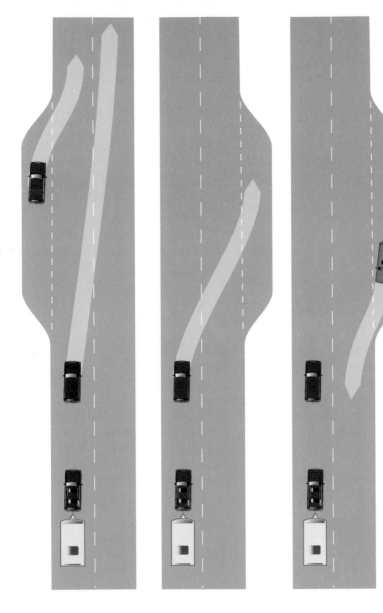

In each of these situations approaching lay-bys, the outfit should beware of overtaking. The arrows show the possible actions of traffic ahead.

Bends, hill crests, hump back bridges and any other aspect of road layout which could obscure your view must be taken into account. Allow for the possibility that there are fast-moving vehicles approaching you on the sections of road you cannot see. Follow the basic rule for overtaking.

- **Identify a gap into which you can return and the point along the road at which you will be able to enter it.**

- **Judge whether you will be able to reach that point before any approaching vehicle, seen or unseen, could come into conflict with you.**

You should have observed the whole stretch of road necessary to complete the manoeuvre, and know that it does not include any other hazards. Look especially for hazards which might cause the vehicles you are overtaking to alter their position. Make full use of road signs and road markings, especially those giving instructions or warning you of hazards ahead.

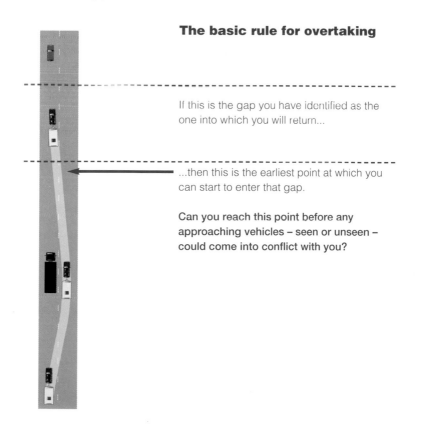

The basic rule for overtaking

If this is the gap you have identified as the one into which you will return...

...then this is the earliest point at which you can start to enter that gap.

Can you reach this point before any approaching vehicles – seen or unseen – could come into conflict with you?

Road surface

The condition of the road surface should always be taken into account before you overtake. There may be ruts or holes which could throw your outfit off course, or surface water which could cause a curtain of spray at a critical moment. The effects of adverse weather on road holding and visibility must always be taken into account.

Overtaking in a stream of vehicles

Overtaking in a stream of vehicles is more difficult because it takes more time. You also have to take into account the possible actions of more drivers both in front and behind. There is always the possibility that drivers in front are not aware of your presence or intention to overtake and that drivers behind might attempt to overtake you.

Before overtaking, you should identify a clear gap between the vehicles in front which you can enter safely. Be aware that the gap may close up before you arrive, so choose gaps that are large enough to allow for this. Do not overtake if you will have to force your vehicle into a gap.

Where a queue has formed because of an obstruction in the road ahead, do not attempt to jump the queue. This invariably annoys other road users and can be dangerous.

Overtaking on a single carriageway

Overtaking on a single carriageway is perhaps the most hazardous form of overtaking. While you are overtaking, your vehicle is in the path of any oncoming vehicles so great care must be taken before deciding on the manoeuvre.

Develop the ability to judge the speed and distance of oncoming vehicles accurately. You need to be able to assess whether you can reach the return gap before they do. Remember you always have the option of deciding not to overtake. Judging the speed of an oncoming vehicle is extremely difficult, especially on long straight roads. The size and type of the approaching vehicle may give you an indication of its possible speed.

Plan and prepare your overtaking carefully. As well as looking for vehicles, train yourself to look specifically for motorcyclists, cyclists and pedestrians before you overtake. If you do not expect to see something, you may not see it when it is there –

an oncoming pedestrian or cyclist can be easily overlooked.

Overtaking on bends

Avoid overtaking on bends in an outfit. Take the opportunity to take views to the offside of the vehicle in front in a right-hand bend, and to the nearside in a left-hand bend. This will help you to assess the opportunites for overtaking in the approaching stretch of straight road.

Single carriageway roads marked with three lanes

Single carriageway roads marked with three lanes are inherently dangerous as the overtaking lane in each direction is the shared centre lane. Never attempt to overtake if there is the possibility of an approaching vehicle moving into the centre lane. Avoid overtaking when you would make a third line of moving vehicles unless you are sure it is absolutely safe to do so.

When you are judging speed and distance to overtake and a vehicle is approaching, look out for the presence of the 'lurker'. This is a vehicle which closes right up behind other vehicles and then sweeps out into full view. Do not assume that the drivers of light vehicles or cars behind a heavy lorry are content to stay where they are. They could well pull out just when you are overtaking.

Overtaking on a dual carriageway

You should always overtake on the right on dual carriageways except when traffic is moving in queues and the queue on the right is moving more slowly than you are. While towing, you may not use the outside lane on dual carriageways (*including motorways*) with three or more lanes, unless there are roadworks or signs that indicate otherwise.

On dual carriageways it can be more difficult to judge the speed of traffic approaching from the rear. Before overtaking watch carefully the vehicles in the nearside lanes. If one of them is closing up on the vehicle in

Avoid the temptation to follow another vehicle through an apparently safe gap on a three-lane single carriageway. Always assess a safe return position for yourself. The leading vehicle may well be able to slip safely into place on the nearside leaving you stranded in the middle faced by oncoming vehicles.

front, the driver may pull out, possibly without signalling or only signalling as the vehicle starts to move out. A good guide is the distance between the wheels of the vehicle and the lane markings. If the gap narrows it could be moving out. Overtaking when it would cause three vehicles to be abreast should be avoided if possible, although on many motorways this is difficult. On fast moving roads anticipate the effects of wind turbulence if you overtake a high-sided vehicle. Do not overtake if you have any qualms about your outfit's stability at that speed.

Overtaking downhill

Avoid overtaking while going downhill in an outfit. The increase in speed and the hill make the outfit susceptible to snaking. Any road surface irregularity or wind buffeting from other traffic could cause your trailer to snake.

Assisting others to overtake

Assisting other road users to overtake eases tensions and improves the quality of driving for everyone on the road. The key element is your attitude of mind when you drive. You should not regard driving as a competition but as a means of travelling between two points as safely as possible. Be aware of traffic building up behind you and leave a sufficient gap between your outfit and the vehicle in front to allow others to overtake. Never travel in tight trailer convoys with inadequate overtaking gaps between the individual outfits. If other drivers wish to overtake, assist them:

● use your mirrors to monitor the build up of traffic behind you and assess whether they wish to overtake or not

● allow enough distance between you and the vehicle in front for vehicles to overtake

● if a queue has built up behind you find a safe opportunity, such as a lay-by, to pull in and let the queue pass.

Check lists, maintenance programmes and further information

Hitching-up check

Each time you hitch up check the following:

- [ ] the noseweight is correct
- [ ] the load is balanced and secure, and any required marker or lighting boards are in place
- [ ] any gates, doors, windows or skylights are locked shut and gas bottles are turned off
- [ ] the towball is adequately greased, unless you are using a towball-mounted friction stabiliser
- [ ] the brake system and the coupling mechanism (do a visual check)
- [ ] the head is locked onto the ball indicated by the position of locking handle or the visual indicator; lower the jockey wheel and raise the towball a couple of winds to test that the head and ball are truly engaged
- [ ] the posture of the trailer is correct – level or slightly down to the hitch
- [ ] the breakaway/secondary coupling is sound and attached to the towing vehicle
- [ ] the electric connectors are plugged into their sockets, and the cables are sound, provide adequate slack for cornering and are clear of the ground
- [ ] the jockey wheel is raised and correctly stowed
- [ ] on older trailers: the manual reverse lever is not engaged
- [ ] the trailer handbrake is off and any prop stands/corner steadies are raised and correctly stowed

- ☐ the tyres are undamaged and correctly inflated (vehicle tyres as well)
- ☐ switch on vehicle ignition and ask an assistant to help check that lights, brakelights and indicators are working on the trailer
- ☐ adjust your wing and rearview mirrors to give you a good view along both sides and behind the trailer
- ☐ check your load and trailer are secure and check the wheel hubs for excess heat 15 minutes after the journey's start and 15 minutes after joining a motorway or fast dual carriageway.

Journey check

Each day or before each new journey check:

- ☐ the noseweight if the load has been altered
- ☐ the hitch is firmly coupled
- ☐ the breakaway/secondary coupling is sound and attached to the towing vehicle
- ☐ the electric connectors are plugged in and the cables are sound
- ☐ the jockey wheel is raised and correctly stowed
- ☐ the tyres are undamaged and correctly inflated
- ☐ the load is balanced and secure, and any required marker or lighting boards are in place
- ☐ any gates, doors, windows or skylights are locked shut and gas bottles are turned off
- ☐ the handbrake is off and any prop stands/corner steadies are raised and correctly stowed
- ☐ your load and trailer 15 minutes after the journey start and 15 minutes after joining a motorway or fast dual carriageway.

And your vehicle check too!

Pre-driving check

Carry out this check every time you get into your vehicle. If it is not your usual vehicle, make sure you are familiar with the position and operation of the controls and instruments, and whether it is fitted with supplementary aids such as ABS before setting off:

☐ handbrake on, gear in neutral

☐ adjust seat (position, rake and height if adjustable) to give good all round vision and good access to the controls

☐ check position of and, if necessary, adjust the mirrors

☐ handbrake and footbrake respond firmly

☐ doors are securely closed.

Switch on ignition, note warning lights; set manual choke if necessary and start engine. Continue with these checks:

☐ after system becomes operational check the instruments; If any of the earlier checks could not be completed before ignition or start up, do them now

☐ carry out stationary brake test to ensure the system is working

☐ check gauges and warning lights

☐ check seat belt – not frayed or twisted, locks when tugged, releases on depressing the button, properly adjusted – and then fit it

☐ check in mirrors, select gear, check over shoulder, release handbrake (in automatics keep footbrake depressed before engaging DRIVE), move off when safe

☐ as soon as possible after moving off carry out a moving brake test. Check the gauges and warning lights at intervals during the journey, and take action if necessary.

Maintenance programmes

Correct maintenance requires constant vigilance. Whenever you have the slightest suspicion that something feels, looks or sounds not quite right investigate it. The regular maintenance programmes are additional to the constant vigilance, not a substitute for it. Where the manufacturer suggests more frequent or additional checks to the ones below, follow the manufacturer's advice. You are generally advised to entrust the annual service and any braking system work to a specialist trailer firm.

Every 2000 miles or 3 months

☐ Check and lubricate the coupling/overrun mechanism and the brake linkages.

☐ Grab each trailer wheel with your hands 180° apart, and rock to check for excessive movement in bearings. Fully service bearing if suspect.

Every 3000 miles

☐ Reset the brake shoes and all the brake linkages – replace brake shoes with warranted parts when their linings reach 2mm thickness.

☐ Repack wheel bearings with grease, except for sealed-for-life units.

After storage

☐ Carry out the 2000 and 3000 mile maintenance programmes.

☐ Carefully inspect tyres for flats, bulges, ageing, wear and tyre pressures.

☐ Carefully inspect electrical connectors for corrosion; burnish connectors if necessary.

☐ Check all trailer lights and indicators are working correctly.

If stored for more than a year, carry out a full annual service.

Annual service

Test, lubricate and service as appropriate:

☐ towbar assembly and fixings

☐ coupling head and locking mechanism

☐ breakaway/secondary coupling cable and anchorage

☐ electrical connectors, cables and exterior fittings

☐ internal gas and electrical fittings and circuits

☐ override mechanism, wheel brake and handbrake mechanisms, auto-reverse mechanism, brake shoes and drums

☐ hubs and bearings

☐ tyres for damage, ageing and tread wear

☐ suspension

☐ chassis and body panels.

Further information

British Rubber Manufacturers' Association Ltd
90 Tottenham Court Road
London W1P 0BR
Telephone 0207 580 2794

Publishers of the booklet *Tyre Tips for Trailers*

The Camping and Caravanning Club
Greenfields House
Westwood Way
Coventry
West Midlands
CV4 8JH
Telephone 01203 694995

The Caravan Club
East Grinstead House
East Grinstead
West Sussex
RH19 1UA
Telephone 01342 326944

The National Trailer and Towing Association Ltd
No 1 Alveston Place
Leamington Spa
Warwickshire
CV4 4SN
Telephone 01926 335445

The Society of Motor Manufacturers and Traders Ltd
Forbes House   *Gersch Weiller*
Halkin Street
London
SW1X 7DS
Telephone 0207 235 7000

Publishers of the booklet *Towing and the Law*

The Trailer and Towing Advisory Service
16 Moore Drive
Helensburgh
Argyll and Bute
G84 7LE
Telephone 01436 678686

Glossary

ABS: See *Antilock braking system*

Acceleration sense: The ability to vary vehicle speed in response to changing road and traffic conditions by accurate use of the accelerator.

Antilock braking system: A braking system which retains the ability to steer during harsh or emergency braking. Also known as ABS.

Aquaplaning: A serious loss of steering and braking control caused by a wedge of water building up between the front tyres and the road surface.

Auto-reverse brakes: Trailer brakes that incorporate a mechanism allowing the trailer to be reversed without activating its brakes.

Blindspots: Areas around a vehicle which the driver cannot see because the bodywork blocks sight or the mirrors do not cover these areas.

Breakaway cable: A cable connected between the towing vehicle and the trailer's braking mechanism. Designed as a safety device to apply the trailer brakes if the trailer should part from the towing vehicle. After applying the brakes, the cable is designed to break, leaving the trailer detached from the towing vehicle, but coming to a halt.

Camber: The convex slope across a road surface designed to assist drainage. Camber falls from the crown of the road to the edges. It has an effect on cornering which differs according to whether the bend is to the right or the left.

Cornering: Cornering is used to mean driving a car round a corner, curve or bend. Its meaning is not restricted to corners.

End swing: As a trailer changes direction going round a corner it pivots about its wheels and swings its end out to the outside of the sweep – make sure there is enough clearance behind and to the outside of a trailer's sweep to avoid hitting any other road user or object.

Engine compression: The compression of gases in the cylinders of an internal combustion engine. Compression uses energy so, when deceleration reduces the fuel supply to the engine, energy for compression is taken from the road wheels, thereby slowing them down.

Engine torque: The turning power developed by an engine.

Following position: The distance at which it is safe to follow a vehicle in front. This distance varies according to the circumstances.

Gross train weight (GTW): The maximum weight a vehicle can move on the road as stated by the vehicle's manufacturer. It includes the vehicle's own maximum authorised mass (MAM) (see below) and the maximum weight of an attached loaded trailer. It is the same as the combined MAM.

Gross vehicle weight (GVW): The total weight of a trailer or towing vehicle and its load.

Hazard/hazardous: Any thing or situation that has the potential for danger.

Information phase: First phase of the system of car control which underlies the other phases. *See Chapter 6*

Kerbweight (KW): There are two definitions of kerbweight. The first is the definition established in UK legislation, the second is the definition used in EU Directives.

Kerbweight (KW) (as defined in Constuction and Use Regulations 1986): The weight of a vehicle as it leaves the manufacturer with a full tank of fuel, adequate fluids for normal operation (lubricants, oils, water etc), and the standard set of tools and equipment as supplied by the manufacturer for that vehicle. It does not include the weight of the driver, occupants or load. For a trailer the KW is the unladen weight of the trailer.

Kerbweight (KW): (as defined by EU Directive 95/48/EC): The weight of a vehicle as it leaves the manufacturer with its fuel tank 90% full, all the necessary fluids for normal operation (lubricants, oils, water etc), a nominal driver weight of 68kg, and 7kg of luggage.

Limit point: The limit point is the furthest point along a road to which you have an uninterrupted view of the road surface. On a level stretch of road this will be where the right-hand side of the road appears to intersect with the left-hand side of the road. The limit point is used in a system of cornering called limit point analysis.

Maximum authorised mass (MAM): The maximum total weight that a vehicle is designed to carry. It is set by the vehicle manufacturer, and includes the vehicle weight and the load carried. It is the same as the older terms: permissible maximum weight and maximum gross weight.

Maximum gross weight: Tthe maximum gross weight set by the manufacturer.

Nearside: The left-hand side of the car and the road from the position of the driving seat facing forward, the opposite to offside.

Noseweight: The weight that the trailer puts on the towball or other coupling mechanism of the towing vehicle.

Offside: The right-hand side of the car and the road from the position of the driving seat facing forward, the opposite to nearside.

Overrun/inertia brakes: A mechanism which applies a trailer's brakes when the towing vehicle brakes. When the towing vehicle brakes, the inertia of the trailer compresses a device in the towbar which activates a series of levers connected by cables to the brakes. The harder the tow vehicle brakes, the firmer the application of the trailer brakes.

Oversteer: The tendency of an outfit to turn more than you would expect for the amount of turn given to the steering wheel.

Overtaking position: The position adopted behind another vehicle in readiness to overtake when a safe opportunity arises. It is closer than the following position and reduces the time you have to react to actions of the vehicle in front. It should only be adopted if you know there are no hazards ahead which might cause the vehicle in front to brake suddenly.

Revs: The number of engine revolutions per minute.

Road users: Any user of the highway: vehicles, cyclists, pedestrians, animals. The term is used to emphasise the need to be aware of everything on the highway, not just vehicles.

Safe stopping distance rule: This rule is one of the basic safety considerations when towing. It controls your speed by relating speed to the ability to stop. Always drive so that you are able to stop on your own side of the road in the distance you can see to be clear.

Scanning: A method of observation. The use of regular visual sweeps of the whole of the driving environment – the distance, the mid-ground, the foreground, sides and rear – to ensure that the driver is aware of everything that is happening.

Secondary coupling: A cable or chain connected between a trailer and the towing vehicle. Designed to prevent the trailer from becoming detached if the main coupling should fail. Also called a safety chain. Only used on small trailers.

Snaking: Swaying of the trailer from side to side to such an extent that it moves the towing vehicle and affects the stability of the outfit as a whole.

Superelevation: Superelevation is the banking up of a section of road towards the outside edge of the curve. This makes the slope favourable for cornering in both directions.

The system – the system of driving control: A systematic way of approaching and negotiating hazards that emphasises safety and is central to *Towing Roadcraft*. It is fully explained in Chapter 6.

Torque: See *Engine torque*

Traction control systems: Traction control improves vehicle stability and assists steering by controlling excess wheel slip on individual wheels and reducing engine power to maintain tyre grip.

Trailer cutting: Trailers do not follow the path of the towing vehicle's front wheels round bends and corners; they take a shorter route. This means they cut across on the inside of the curve taken by the towing vehicle's wheels, causing the trailer wheels to mount kerbs avoided by the vehicle. The tighter the curve the more pronounced the trailer cutting. When towing round a tight curve allow space on the inside of the curve for this to happen.

Tyre grip trade-off: The tyre grip available in any given situation is limited, and is shared between accelerating, braking and steering forces. If more of the tyre grip is used for braking or accelerating, less will be available for steering.

Undertaking: Overtaking on the nearside in situations which contravene the *Highway Code*.

Unladen weight: The weight of a vehicle or trailer including its body and any parts normally used with it when working on a road. This does not include the weight of fuel, water or batteries used for moving the vehicle, or the weight of loose equipment or tools.

Index

Index